PENGUIN BOOKS

Noodle

BIBLE

D1399936

Noodle

BIBLE

Jacki Passmore

Contents

Introduction

In Asia, noodles compete with rice as the staple food in every cuisine except Indian. In western countries, the demand for noodles just keeps growing. And for good reason: noodles are the ultimate in convenience food. They are healthy, inexpensive to buy, and nothing could be quicker or easier to cook.

This book offers a feast of noodle recipes from all corners of Asia and Southeast Asia as well as 'east meets west' dishes. It also tells you everything you need to know about choosing, storing, cooking and serving noodles, and preparing garnishes and side dishes. Simple or sumptuous — it's all here.

Noodle basics

You don't need anything in the way of special equipment for cooking noodles: a large, deep saucepan or wok; a wire basket for immersing the noodles; and a colander or strainer for draining them.

In the pantry, a supply of basic Asian spices, sauces, and ingredients such as coconut milk will allow you to put together a meal in no time at all. And while I've provided recipes for home-made stocks, commercial dashi, chicken, fish and beef stock (boxed, powder, granules or cubes) are a perfectly acceptable substitute when you're short of time.

Finally, have all the ingredients and sauces ready before you begin to cook, and plan to serve as soon as the dish is ready. And that's really about all you need to worry about!

Types of noodles

Tradition, taste preference, aesthetics, and cooking requirements all play a part in the choice of noodles for a dish. The Chinese have traditionally enjoyed wheat noodles made with egg; Vietnamese prefer rice noodles; the Japanese – avid noodle eaters – enjoy plump wheat noodles (*udon*) and the nutty-tasting buckwheat *soba*, and they can't resist the Chinese noodles they call *ramen*.

Certain noodles are best in liquid dishes, while others respond to frying in oil by crisping to a pleasing crunch. Chewy, meaty noodles serve some recipes best; others need no more than wisps of soft noodle, providing textural contrast. I have specified a particular style of noodle for each of these recipes, but I wouldn't discourage you from experimenting within the framework of the recipe.

It has to be said that I cannot see the point in making fresh noodles at home when bought ones take just a few minutes to cook. Fresh noodles are now readily available, in supermarkets as well as Asian food stores, and they keep well

in the freezer. I always keep both fresh and dried rice and wheat noodles on hand. But it's not difficult to make your own noodle dough: for a recipe, see page 241.

BEAN-THREAD (OR CELLOPHANE) NOODLES

Made from mung beans or broad beans. When cooked they are slippery and near transparent, with an enjoyable bite. Occasionally used in stir-fried dishes but more often in soups, hot pots and braised dishes. Also known as bean threads or glass noodles.

CHINESE EGG NOODLES

The classic Chinese noodle, made from a flour-and-egg dough and sold in bundles. Thin egg noodles are typically used for soups and stir-fries. Fat egg noodles are about 3 mm wide and therefore require slightly longer cooking than the thin variety, and (although the preparation process is the same) they have a slightly different flavour.

Hokkien mee: Thick egg and wheat-flour noodles resembling

spaghetti but coloured bright yellow with food dye. Fresh *hokkien mee* are sold by weight and have been dipped in oil. Rinse with boiling water before adding to a dish.

JAPANESE NOODLES

Many Japanese recipes can be made with the noodles of your choice. Most soup noodles are interchangeable.

Hiyamugi: Fine white noodles similar to somen and used specifically in cold dishes.

Sukiyaki noodles (shirataki): The noodles used in sukiyaki. Made from a root vegetable that grows readily in Japan, they are produced by the same extrusion method applied to bean-thread vermicelli, which can replace them in a recipe. *Shirataki* noodles packed in water in a plastic tube are easy to use but less economical than dried noodles.

Soba: Round stick noodles, grey or buff in colour, that are made from buckwheat flour. They have a pleasing taste and texture quite unlike other forms of noodle; if unobtainable,

use Japanese somen or other wheat-flour noodles. *Cha-soba* are flavoured and coloured with green tea.

Somen: Thin, white stick noodles made from hard-wheat flour, water and oil. They are packed similarly to soba, in straight bundles bound with ribbon. They are quite breakable, so handle with care or they'll crumble. Substitute wheat noodles, or spaghettini.

Udon: Plump noodles made with hard wheat flour, salt and water, available in supermarkets. Used in soups and hot pots.

RICE NOODLES

Available in most Asian food stores, rice noodle dough sheets can be cut to the width you require, and can also be filled for steaming as rice rolls. They will keep fresh for only a few days in the refrigerator.

Dried rice-stick noodles: In the pack they look like milky plastic extrusions; they turn soft and white when cooked. Sticks vary in width, and marginally in taste, from brand to brand.

In Vietnam they are called *banh pho*, and in Thailand *sen mie*. Keep dry in storage, and do not overcook or they will fall apart. Narrow (thin) Vietnamese rice sticks are known as *bun* and are very white when cooked.

Fresh rice ribbon noodles: Available (chilled) in Asian food stores and some supermarkets, these noodles should be rinsed in hot water and require minimal cooking.

Rice vermicelli: Sold in flat bundles, usually five to a pack. The thin, cream-coloured strands turn white when soaked or cooked in water, and expand dramatically to a frothy white cloud when deep-fried. Again, make sure they stay dry in storage.

WHEAT NOODLES

White noodles (such as somen) made with hard wheat flour, salt and water. They are more fragile in texture than egg noodles, which they can replace in any recipe. They may be thin, flat or ribbon-like.

Cooking and storing noodles

Bring a large pan of water to the boil, with or without salt as you prefer. When the water is briskly bubbling, add the noodles with 2–3 teaspoons of vegetable oil to prevent them sticking together. Stir with chopsticks to untangle them. Return the water to a brisk boil, begin to time cooking at this point, and slightly reduce the heat so the water continues to boil but is not bubbling fiercely. Remove noodles as soon as they are done – al dente, of course. Drain well and rinse with hot water if starchy.

I have given specific instructions for cooking the noodles in most of the recipes. The principles are simple: you can cook all noodles in advance and reheat by placing them in a deep wire basket and immersing in a pot of briskly boiling water. Or, if you prefer, put them in a microwave dish, cover with plastic wrap and microwave on high, until heated through. It is advisable to sprinkle a little cold water over the surface of the noodles before microwaving.

It is impossible to be absolutely accurate when recommending cooking times (anywhere from 3 to 8 minutes), as the quality of packaged dried noodles varies considerably and will affect times. Fresh noodles rarely require more than 3½ minutes to cook, unless they have been allowed to dry out, when they will need longer.

COOKING TIMES FOR AL DENTE NOODLES

The times are calculated from when the water returns to the boil after adding the noodles.

· dried (Chinese) egg noodles (thin/regular), ramen and flavoured noodles	3½ minutes (4–4½ minutes if in tight bundles)
· dried (Chinese) egg noodles (medium)	5 minutes
· dried (Chinese) egg noodles (flat)	6–8½ minutes, depending on thickness
· dried soba noodles	3 minutes
· dried udon noodles	5½–6 minutes
· dried rice sticks (narrow)	3 minutes (3½–4½ minutes for medium to wide)

- dried rice vermicelli $1\frac{1}{2}$ minutes
- dried bean-thread vermicelli $1\frac{1}{2}$ minutes
- dried, very fine wheat
  noodles (somen, miswa) $1\frac{1}{2}-2$ minutes
- dried, flat wheat noodles $3-3\frac{1}{2}$ minutes (6 minutes
  (narrow) for wide)
- fresh egg noodles (narrow) $2-2\frac{1}{2}$ minutes ($3\frac{1}{2}-4$
  minutes if flat and wide)

- fresh rice ribbon or
  rice stick noodles 30 seconds
- fresh hokkien mee 3–4 minutes
- fresh udon $2\frac{1}{2}$ minutes

For some recipes, bean-thread and rice vermicelli are soaked, not cooked. Soaking times are as follows:

- in hot water 9 minutes
- in boiling water 3–4 minutes
- in cold water 25 minutes

JAPANESE METHOD FOR COOKING NOODLES

Udon and soba: Bring 2 litres of water to a brisk boil. Add the noodles and stir slowly to prevent them from sticking. When the water returns to the boil, add ½–1 cup cold water and bring to the boil again. Add another ½–1 cup cold water and return to the boil. Reduce heat and cook the noodles for about 2½ minutes, or until al dente. Drain, pour the noodles into a pan of cold water, and stir to arrest cooking and remove starch. Drain and set aside, then reheat before serving.

Somen: Bring 1.5 litres of water to the boil. Add the noodles, bring back to the boil, and cook for 30 seconds. Add ½ cup cold water and bring back to the boil. Do this two more times (using 1½ cups cold water in all), each time bringing the water back to the boil. Then cook until the noodles are al dente. Drain in a colander.

Wheat noodles cooked in this way should be used at once. Do not soak in cold water or they will lose their texture.

Soaking noodles

Bean-thread vermicelli, rice vermicelli and fresh rice ribbons are simply soaked to soften, in hot or boiling water.

Place the noodles in a bowl, pour the water over, and set aside until the noodles have softened to the required consistency. In boiling water they will take 3–4 minutes; in hot water, 8–9 minutes; and in cold water, 25 minutes. Noodles that are to be cooked (e.g. stir-fried) or added to a hot soup should still be slightly firm when they come out of the water.

Storing noodles

Dried noodles will keep pretty much indefinitely if stored in an airtight container.

Use fresh noodles within two or three days if storing them in the refrigerator. This particularly applies to the thick, round, yellow noodles that have been coated with oil. Fresh noodles also freeze well: thaw them in the fridge before using.

Cooked noodles freeze well. Pour drained noodles into plastic bags, each containing one or two servings, then freeze. Reheat in boiling water, or microwave on high.

Special stocks

Because many of their dishes are cooked for a short time only, Asian cooks rely on well-flavoured stocks to give soups and sauces the required depth and complexity of taste. I usually make stock in large quantities: you can freeze it in convenient 1–2-cup quantities so you always have a ready supply. It can be thawed in the microwave, or overnight in the refrigerator.

For Chinese and Malaysian dishes, a rich pork stock and a well flavoured chicken stock are most important. Vietnamese dishes need these, plus an intense beef stock fragrant with anise and cassia or lemongrass. Japanese dishes need only dashi (an infusion of dried fish and seaweed).

To make Asian-style pork, chicken or vegetable stock, simply add 1–2 spring onions and a 2-cm piece of fresh ginger to the pot with the other stock ingredients. (For Thai and Vietnamese dishes, also add 2 stems of lemongrass.)

< Ichiban dashi (dashi stock: page 18)

Ichiban dashi (dashi stock)

1 litre cold water
15 g kombu seaweed
15 g dried bonito flakes

Pour the water into a saucepan and add the kombu. Bring slowly to the boil, removing the kombu just before the bubbles begin to break. Retain the kombu for further use. Add the bonito flakes, bring quickly to the boil, then remove immediately from the heat. Allow the bonito to settle in the stock for 1 minute, then strain through a sieve lined with a piece of fine cloth.

Ichiban dashi is used for clear soups, when clarity of colour and a delicate but well-defined taste are required. The heavier stock Niban dashi is used for strong-flavoured soups, sauces and simmered dishes: kombu and bonito reused from Ichiban dashi are simmered in water until liquid is reduced by half, then extra bonito flakes are added for just a minute before the stock is strained.

MAKES 1 LITRE

Japanese noodle broth

2 litres ichiban dashi (page 18)

2½ tablespoons dark soy sauce

¼ cup light soy sauce

2 tablespoons sugar

2½ tablespoons mirin
   (Japanese sweet rice wine)

salt to taste

Combine all ingredients in a large saucepan and bring to the boil.
Simmer for 1 minute, then strain. Use immediately, or make in
advance and refrigerate for 2 to 3 days.

MAKES 2 LITRES

Aromatic beef stock

2 medium-sized onions,
    unpeeled

2 cloves garlic, unpeeled

1 kg gravy beef, cut
    into 5-cm cubes

1 kg beef bones, preferably ribs

2 ham hocks

3 litres water

3 whole star anise

1 cinnamon stick

1 × 5-cm piece fresh ginger,
    peeled and quartered

Preheat the oven to 200°C. Place onions, garlic, beef and beef bones
on a large oven tray and roast for 25–30 minutes.

Bring a pot of water (enough to cover the hocks) to the boil. Place the
hocks in a bowl, add the water, steep for 5 minutes, then drain.

Transfer the hocks to a large saucepan and add the contents of the oven
tray. Add the 3 litres of water and the spices and ginger. Bring to the boil,
reduce the heat, and skim the surface. Place a lid on the pot, allowing a
small opening for steam to escape. Simmer with the water barely bubbling
for at least 2¼ hours. Strain into containers and cool quickly over iced
water, then refrigerate or freeze.

MAKES ABOUT 2 LITRES

Soup noodles

Soup noodles are hard to resist. What could be more nourishing and satisfying than a big bowl of tender-chewy wheat or rice noodles with tender slivers of chicken or fish, scarlet prawns, jade-green leafy vegetables in a clear soup, or a creamy, curry-flavoured laksa broth?

Soup noodles are a treat to enjoy from breakfast through to a late-night pick-me-up. They're fast and easy to prepare, and quite simply delicious.

< Indonesian chicken noodle soup (page 24)

Indonesian chicken noodle soup

1.5 kg chicken thighs

3 cups water

2 thick slices fresh ginger

salt and white pepper

500 g hokkien noodles

150 g fresh bean sprouts,
  blanched

2 tablespoons diagonally
  sliced spring onions
  (green parts only)

2 tablespoons fried onion flakes
  (page 237)

hot chilli sauce, to serve

2 tablespoons coriander seeds

1 teaspoon cumin seeds

½ teaspoon aniseed
  or caraway seeds

1 tablespoon chopped galangal
  or fresh ginger

3 tablespoons chopped shallots
  or onion

3 large cloves garlic, peeled

2 tablespoons chopped
  macadamia nuts

3 tablespoons peanut or
  vegetable oil

Place chicken in a saucepan with the water and the ginger. Bring to the boil, reduce the heat to low, and simmer for about 30 minutes.

Meanwhile, make the *rempah*. Roast the coriander, cumin and aniseed in a dry pan over medium heat until aromatic. Transfer to a spice grinder and grind to a powder. Add the galangal or ginger, shallots, garlic and macadamia nuts, and grind to a reasonably smooth paste (add a little of the oil if blades begin to clog). Heat the oil in another pan over medium heat and fry the spice paste for about 4 minutes, until aromatic.

Remove chicken from broth, drain briefly and then fry with the rempah until well coloured. Strain the broth into another pan, add the chicken and continue to cook until very tender (about 30 minutes). Skim the fat from the broth, remove the chicken, debone and tear flesh into pieces. Season the broth with salt and pepper to taste.

Cook the noodles in boiling water for about 2½ minutes (if using spaghetti, cook for 12–13 minutes) until al dente. Drain well. Divide among soup bowls and place chicken on top. Pour the sauce over, and add bean sprouts. Garnish with the spring onions and onion flakes. Serve a hot chilli sauce on the side.

Most Malaysian and Indonesian dishes begin with an aromatic blend of fresh herbs and dried spices, ground by hand in a stone mortar. This is the *rempah*, the secret to the wonderful depth of flavour found in these dishes.

SERVES 4 (6–8 IF SHARING SEVERAL DISHES)

Vermicelli in clear soup
with cha siu

225 g dried fine wheat vermicelli,
  or somen noodles

275 g cha siu (Chinese roast
  pork: page 230), thinly sliced

6 dried shiitake mushrooms,
  soaked for 20 minutes in
  warm water

7 cups chicken stock

1 tablespoon rice wine or
  dry sherry

1 teaspoon shredded
  fresh ginger

3 stems Asian greens
  (e.g. choy sum or gai larn),
  cut into 5-cm pieces

1½ tablespoons light soy sauce

salt and white pepper

2–3 tablespoons diagonally
  sliced spring-onion greens

Bring 1.5 litres water to the boil and salt sparingly. Add noodles, return to boil, reduce heat and simmer until the noodles are tender (about 1½ minutes). Drain, then distribute noodles among six soup bowls and set aside.

Drain the mushrooms and remove and discard the stems. In a large saucepan bring stock to the boil, add the wine, ginger, mushrooms and Asian greens, and simmer for 5–7 minutes until vegetables are tender. Season with soy sauce and add salt and pepper to taste.

Pour stock over the noodles, placing equal amounts of vegetables in each bowl. Add the sliced pork on top, and garnish with spring-onion greens.

SERVES 6

Chicken & seafood soup noodles

175 g dried fine wheat vermicelli, or somen noodles

125 g fresh, cleaned squid

100 g green (raw) prawns, shelled and deveined

100 g poached boneless, skinless chicken or boiled pork

6 cups fish stock

1 teaspoon sugar

1 cup fresh bean sprouts

1 cup shredded Chinese cabbage

2–3 teaspoons light soy sauce

½ cup finely sliced spring-onion greens

a few sprigs fresh coriander

lime wedges

Bring 1.5 litres water to the boil, add the noodles and cook for 1 minute. Remove from heat and leave to stand for 1 minute more, then drain.

Cut the squid into rings. Slice the prawns in half lengthways. Slice the chicken or pork, stack the slices together, and cut into fine shreds.

Bring the stock to the boil, add the sugar, squid, prawns, bean sprouts and cabbage, and cook for 2 minutes. Season with soy sauce. Add the noodles and heat through, then ladle into bowls.

Arrange a little stack of the shredded meat on the noodles, garnish with the spring onions and coriander, and serve with lime wedges for squeezing into the soup to taste.

To make squid curl into attractive pine-cone shapes when cooked, flatten out the body and score the inside surface in a cross-hatch pattern, without cutting all the way through the flesh. Then cut into squares before cooking.

SERVES 4–6

Seafood coconut curry soup

275 g firm white fish

100 g cleaned squid

100 g fresh scallops or clams

100 g raw (green) prawns,
    shelled and deveined
    (or use crab meat)

200 g dried rice vermicelli

1½ cups fresh bean sprouts

5 spring onions, trimmed
    and finely sliced

sprigs of coriander and mint
    or basil

2–3 tablespoons freshly squeezed
    lime juice, to taste

SOUP

2 large onions, finely sliced

3 tablespoons vegetable oil

1½ teaspoons minced garlic

2 teaspoons minced fresh ginger

1½ teaspoons shrimp paste

½ cup mild Malaysian
    curry paste

2 fresh green chillies,
    deseeded and finely sliced

1½ cups thick coconut milk

5 cups water

salt and freshly ground pepper

Cut the fish into 5-mm cubes, and the squid into rings or scored squares (see note page 29). Slice the scallops in half horizontally; clams can be left in their shells after a thorough scrub with a brush.

Soften the noodles in hot water for 3½ minutes and drain well. Bring a small pan of water to the boil, add the bean sprouts, blanch for 30 seconds, and drain. Refresh in cold water, drain again, and set aside. >

To make the soup, sauté the sliced onions in the oil over medium heat until soft and translucent, remove and reserve half, and continue cooking the remainder until well browned. Add the garlic, ginger and shrimp paste, and cook, stirring, for 1 minute. Pour in the curry sauce, add the chillies and cook over medium heat for 5 minutes, stirring. Pour in the coconut milk and bring to the boil, stirring. Reduce heat and cook gently for about 12 minutes.

Add the 5 cups water, bring to the boil again, then reduce heat and simmer for 10 minutes. Return the reserved onions and add the seafood. Bring to the boil and simmer gently for a few minutes. Check seasoning, adding salt and pepper to taste.

When ready to serve, bring about 2 litres water to the boil. Place the spring onions and herbs in little dishes, and the lime juice in small bowls.

Place the noodles in a strainer and pour the boiling water over to reheat, then drain well and divide evenly among soup bowls. Place some bean sprouts on top of the noodles. Pour the hot soup over, distributing the seafood evenly among the bowls. Serve with the condiments, for each diner to add.

SERVES 4–8

Five-minute noodle soup with Chinese sausage

100 g dried rice vermicelli

2–3 lap cheong (Chinese sausages: see page 246)

5½ cups chicken stock

1 tablespoon canned, salt-preserved vegetables
(turnip or Shanghai cabbage)

1 tablespoon light soy sauce

2 tablespoons minced spring-onion greens

Soak the vermicelli in warm water to soften. Drain. Steam the sausages for 2–3 minutes, remove, and slice diagonally.

Bring the stock to the boil in a large pot and add the sausage. Finely shred the vegetables and add to the pot with the noodles and soy sauce. Serve in deep bowls, garnished with the spring-onion greens.

SERVES 4

Rice noodles & meatballs in soup

325 g stewing beef
(e.g. gravy beef)

1 tablespoon grated fresh ginger

1 teaspoon five-spice powder

1 teaspoon salt

3 tablespoons cornflour

2 egg whites

150 g dried rice-stick noodles

5 cups beef stock

12 spinach leaves or small
lettuce leaves

salt and freshly ground
black pepper

2 tablespoons chopped
spring-onion greens

1 tablespoon shredded
bamboo shoots

1 tablespoon chopped fresh
coriander leaves

Cut the beef into small cubes and place in a food processor with the ginger, five-spice powder, salt, cornflour and egg whites. Process to a smooth paste, then add 3 tablespoons of cold water to make a voluminous, smooth mass.

Bring 2 litres of salted water to the boil. Drop spoonfuls of the beef mixture into the bubbling water and cook until they rise to the surface (about 2½ minutes). Cook for another 1 minute, then remove with slotted spoon and set aside. **>**

In the same pot of water, cook the noodles for about 3 minutes, until tender. Using a wire ladle, transfer the noodles directly to soup bowls. Discard the cooking water and rinse the pan.

Bring the stock to the boil in the rinsed-out pot. Add spinach and check seasonings, adding salt and pepper to taste. Pour soup over the noodles, divide the meatballs among the bowls, and garnish with the spring onions, bamboo shoots and coriander. Have fish and chilli sauces on the table for your guests to add to their bowls, as desired.

You can make a batch of these meatballs when you have a little spare beef. They can be poached and then frozen, for a convenient quick meal. Grill them to serve in rice papers, with salad and cold rice vermicelli, or drop into a noodle soup.

SERVES 4 (6 IF SHARING SEVERAL DISHES)

Vietnamese chicken noodle soup

225 g dried thin rice-stick
   noodles

2.25 litres chicken stock

2 chicken legs or thighs

100 g skinless chicken
   breast fillet

1½ cups sliced bamboo shoots

1½ tablespoons fish sauce

2 tablespoons minced
   spring onions

salt and white pepper

chopped fresh coriander leaves

Bring 1.5 litres water to the boil, add the rice sticks, cook for about 3½ minutes and drain.

In another pan bring the chicken stock to the boil, add the chicken legs or thighs, cover and cook gently for 15 minutes, then add the breast meat and cook for a further 15 minutes until tender. Remove the chicken from the broth. Skin and debone the legs or thighs, and tear or cut the meat into small pieces. Slice the chicken breast very thinly.

Reheat the noodles by immersing in a pan of boiling water, then remove and divide among six bowls. Strain the broth and return it to the pan. Return the chicken to the broth and add the remaining ingredients. Heat briefly and check seasonings, adding more salt and fish sauce as needed, then pour over the noodles and serve.

SERVES 6

Vietnamese pho
(aromatic beef noodles)

2 litres aromatic beef stock
(page 20)

3 tablespoons fish sauce

325 g dried rice vermicelli

2 tablespoons vegetable oil

450 g beef fillet, very
thinly sliced

1 onion, thinly sliced

2 cups fresh bean sprouts

ACCOMPANIMENTS

¾ cup finely sliced
spring onions

¼ cup chopped fresh coriander

¼ cup small mint leaves

3 tablespoons hoisin sauce

1–2 fresh red chillies, deseeded
and sliced

Bring stock to boil and flavour to taste with fish sauce. Place the vermicelli
in a bowl and pour boiling water over to generously cover. Let stand for
3 minutes, then drain. Divide the noodles between six deep bowls.

Heat a wok or frying-pan over very high heat and add the oil. Stir-fry the
beef for no more than about 45 seconds, then remove. Add the onion and
stir-fry until golden-brown. Place some of the meat and onion in each bowl
of noodles.

Blanch the bean sprouts in boiling water for 20 seconds and divide among
the bowls. Pour the broth over the noodles. Take the bowls to the table,
with the accompaniments in small dishes.

SERVES 6

Saigon soup

225 g dried rice-stick noodles

175 g skinless chicken
   breast fillet

175 g lean pork

about 3 tablespoons fish sauce

6 large raw (green) prawns,
   shelled and deveined

½ teaspoon chopped garlic

3 tablespoons thinly
   sliced shallots

2 tablespoons vegetable oil

½ stalk celery, finely sliced
   diagonally

7 cups chicken stock

12 leaves water spinach, washed
   and torn in half

½ cup finely sliced
   spring onions

¼ cup chopped roasted peanuts

nuoc cham (Vietnamese sauce:
   page 235)

pickled carrot

Bring at least 2 litres water to the boil, add the noodles, and cook for
3–3½ minutes until barely tender, then drain. Slice the chicken and pork
wafer-thin and season with 2 teaspoons of the fish sauce. Cut the prawns
in half lengthways.

Brown the garlic and shallots in oil over medium heat without allowing them
to burn (about 8 minutes). Drain well and set aside. Sauté the celery briefly
in the same oil, then remove. Add the chicken and pork to the pan and stir-
fry over very high heat for about 1½ minutes, then add the prawns and
sauté until they change colour. >

Heat the stock in another pan and add 2½ tablespoons of the fish sauce. Add the noodles and warm through, then add the cooked chicken, pork, prawns, celery, water spinach and spring onions. Heat briefly. Ladle into bowls and scatter the roasted peanuts, garlic and fried shallots over the top.

Serve with small dishes of nuoc cham (page 235) and shredded pickled carrot.

SERVES 6

Vegetable soup noodles

50 g dried rice-stick noodles

25 g bean-thread vermicelli

1 small Chinese cabbage

1 cup small cauliflower florets

2 cups vegetable stock or water

1 medium carrot, peeled
and sliced

1½ tablespoons vegetable oil

4 spring onions, white parts cut
into 2.5-cm pieces (shred and
reserve the green tops)

½ cup sliced bamboo shoots

¼ cup sliced straw or
oyster mushrooms

25 g fresh bean sprouts

½ cup cubed soft tofu

BROTH

5 cups vegetable stock or water

3 teaspoons dark soy sauce

1½ tablespoons light soy sauce

salt and freshly ground
black pepper

Bring 3 cups water to the boil, add the rice sticks and boil until tender. Drain, rinse under running cold water, and set aside. Soak the bean-thread vermicelli in hot water for 7 minutes to soften.

Cut the cabbage stem into 2.5-cm lengths and chop the leaves coarsely. Heat the vegetable stock or water, and blanch the cabbage stems with the cauliflower for 2 minutes, then remove, reserving the stock. ❯

Heat the oil in a wok over high heat. Stir-fry the carrot slices for 1 minute and remove. Add the drained cabbage stems and cauliflower florets, and the spring onions, and stir-fry for 1 minute. Add the bamboo shoots and straw mushrooms and stir-fry for another minute.

Pour the broth ingredients, plus the stock used for cooking the cabbage and cauliflower, into a pot and bring to the boil. Add the blanched vegetables and simmer until tender. Check the seasonings, then add the rice sticks, vermicelli, cabbage leaves, bean sprouts and tofu. Warm through and serve.

SERVES 6

Egg flowers in crab-flavoured noodle soup

100 g dried rice vermicelli
    or thin egg noodles

75 g fresh bean sprouts

225 g cooked crab meat, flaked

3 teaspoons rice wine or
    dry sherry

1 teaspoon ginger juice
    (see note page 49)

2 spring onions, white parts
    only, minced

light soy sauce, to serve

Chinese red vinegar, to serve

BROTH

6 cups chicken stock

1½ teaspoons salt

1 tablespoon light soy sauce

3 egg whites

Soak the rice vermicelli in warm water for about 8 minutes to soften.
(If using egg or shrimp-flavoured noodles, cook in boiling water for about
5 minutes.)

Rinse the bean sprouts, blanch in simmering water for 30 seconds, then
refresh in cold water and drain. Combine the crab meat with the wine and
ginger juice and set aside.

To make the broth, bring stock to boil in a non-aluminium pan, and add the
salt and soy sauce. Reduce the heat so that the soup is no longer bubbling.

Beat the egg whites and strain to remove filaments. Stir the soup in a circular motion, then slowly pour in the beaten egg in a thin stream. As it cooks it will form fine white threads in the soup.

Add the noodles, crab meat, bean sprouts and spring onions, and heat through. Guests can add soy sauce or vinegar to taste.

If you pinch the cream-coloured seed pods and the tapering root ends off bean sprouts you are left with 'silver sprouts'. Their flavour becomes more subtle, and the elegance they add to a dish makes it worth the extra few minutes' work.

SERVES 4 (6 IF SHARING DISHES)

Fish two ways in noodle soup

600 g white fish, skin removed

1 teaspoon ginger juice
(see note page 49)

2 teaspoons rice wine or
dry sherry

½ teaspoon salt

1¼ teaspoons finely grated
fresh ginger

extra ½ teaspoon salt

2 tablespoons cold water

⅓ cup cornflour

200 g thin wheat noodles

7 cups fish stock

1½ teaspoon salt

½ cup very finely shredded
fresh ginger

Slice two-thirds of the fish thinly, sprinkle with the ginger juice, the wine or sherry, and the salt, and set aside. Cube the remaining fish and grind in a food processor with the grated ginger and extra salt, 1½ tablespoons of the cornflour, and cold water. With wet hands, form the mixture into small balls.

Bring a pan of lightly salted water to the boil, cook the noodles until barely tender, drain, and rinse in cold water. Pour the fish stock into another pan and bring to the boil over medium–high heat. Drop in the fish balls and cook until they float to the surface (about 2 minutes). Add the salt and shredded ginger. Simmer briefly.

Mix the remaining cornflour with ⅓ cup cold water, pour into the broth and stir until it boils and begins to thicken. Add the sliced fish and poach until flesh turns white.

Reheat the noodles in boiling water and drain thoroughly. Divide among six bowls (or transfer to a soup tureen) and pour the hot broth over. Divide the sliced fish, fish balls and ginger shreds evenly between the bowls.

Ginger juice is a more subtle seasoning than ginger flesh itself; it adds a hint of exotic flavour to seafood. To make it, grate fresh ginger onto a square of fine, clean cloth. Gather the edges of the cloth together so the grated ginger forms a ball in the centre, then twist the cloth to extract the juice from the ginger. You will need a 2.5-cm piece of young, fresh ginger to make 1 teaspoon of juice. Older ginger – which is drier and has woody flesh – will yield less: use a 5-cm piece and, if needed, moisten the grated flesh with warm water before squeezing.

SERVES 6 (MORE IF SHARING DISHES)

Short & long soup (wonton & noodle soup)

WONTONS

18 wonton wrappers

100 g fatty pork (e.g. belly)

225 g shelled and deveined prawns

1 egg white

⅔ teaspoon salt

¼ teaspoon white pepper

⅓ teaspoon sesame oil

50 g water chestnuts, very finely chopped

1½ tablespoons very finely chopped garlic chives

SOUP

50 g egg noodles

1.5 litres chicken stock

1 small bunch water spinach or other Asian greens

⅓ teaspoon sesame oil

¼ cup sliced spring-onion greens

light soy sauce and salt to taste

Cover wonton wrappers with a cloth to prevent them from drying out. Have ready a small dish of water.

In a food processor grind the pork, prawns, egg white, salt, pepper and sesame oil to a smooth paste. Add the water chestnuts and garlic chives, and process briefly to combine.

Place a spoonful of the filling in the centre of each wonton wrapper and brush the edges with water. Fold to form a triangle, then bring the two outer points together and pinch to secure them. ➤

Bring a pan of lightly salted water to the boil. Add the wontons in batches of 6 and poach until they float, then cook for another 2 minutes. Remove to a dish of cold water, using a slotted spoon. Cook the remaining wontons.

Boil the noodles in lightly salted water until tender, then drain.

To make the soup, bring the stock to the boil, season to taste with sesame oil, soy sauce and salt, and reduce heat slightly. Cut stems from spinach, and discard or reserve for another recipe. Blanch leaves in boiling water for 10 seconds, drain, and add to the soup. Add the wontons and noodles, and heat through. Pour into a soup tureen or divide between bowls, add spring-onion greens, and serve.

You can buy wonton wrappers (chilled or frozen) in Asian food stores and some supermarkets.

SERVES 6

Combination soup noodles

6 cups pork stock

1 fresh red chilli, deseeded

2 teaspoons vegetable oil

2 tablespoons light soy sauce

1 teaspoon sugar

¾ teaspoon salt

⅓ teaspoon pepper

100 g dried hokkien noodles
(or 450 g fresh)

50 g rice vermicelli

150 g fresh bean sprouts

50 g spinach or water
spinach leaves

225 g green (raw) prawns,
shelled and deveined

75 g cleaned squid, cut
into rings

75 g boiled or roasted pork,
thinly sliced

1½ tablespoons chopped fresh
coriander

2 tablespoons fried onion flakes
(page 237)

roasted chilli flakes
(see note page 54)

Measure the stock into a pan and add the chilli and oil. Simmer over
medium heat for 5–6 minutes, covered. Add the soy sauce, sugar, salt
and pepper, reduce the heat to low, and keep the soup hot until needed.

Bring 1 litre water to the boil. Cook the noodles to al dente and pour into a
colander to drain. Rinse under running cold water and drain again. Leave in
the colander.   >

Cover the rice vermicelli with hot water to soften, let stand for 7 minutes, then drain. Bring a kettle of water to the boil. Pour over the hokkien noodles to reheat through, drain, and divide among soup bowls. Place a portion of the rice vermicelli on top.

Bring the broth to the boil, add the bean sprouts and spinach, and blanch for 30 seconds, then add the prawns, squid and pork, and heat thoroughly. Pour over the noodles and sprinkle on the coriander, and the onion and chilli flakes.

Roasted chilli flakes are a useful garnish. Wrap several large dried red chillies in a piece of aluminium foil and place in a hot oven, over a low gas flame, or in a small, heavy pan over medium heat. Cook until the chillies are dry, crisp and well browned. Crush in a mortar, cool, and store in an airtight spice jar. For roasted chilli powder, grind the roasted chillies in a blender or spice grinder.

SERVES 4 (6–8 IF SHARING SEVERAL DISHES)

Singapore seafood noodle soup

225 g white fish

2 fish heads and bones, or
350 g prawn heads and shells

1 spring onion, trimmed and
cut into 5-cm lengths

1 × 2.5-cm piece fresh ginger

7 cups water

1½ teaspoons salt

100 g thin egg noodles or
shrimp-flavoured noodles

75 g cleaned squid

75 g green (raw) prawns,
shelled and deveined

2 baby bok choy

1 cup sliced Chinese cabbage

4 thin slices fresh ginger,
finely shredded

1½ teaspoons sesame oil

½ cup diced seedless cucumber

½ teaspoon five-spice powder

1 tablespoon light soy sauce

150 g cha siu (Chinese roast
pork: page 230)

75 g fresh bean sprouts

¼ cup fried onion flakes
(page 237)

sprigs of fresh coriander

To prepare the broth, cut fish into cubes, place in a pan with the fish heads and carcasses (or prawn heads and shells), sliced spring onion, the piece of ginger, 7 cups of water, and salt, and bring barely to the boil. Reduce heat and simmer, covered, for 10 minutes (do not allow the water to bubble, as this will cloud the broth). Strain into another pan and keep hot. **>**

Bring 1.5 litres of water to the boil, add the noodles, and cook until tender (about 5½ minutes). Drain, rinse in hot water, and drain again.

Cut the squid into 5-cm squares. Cut the bok choy in half lengthways, blanch for 2 minutes in lightly salted water, and drain.

Add the squid, prawns, bok choy, cabbage, shredded ginger, and sesame oil to the broth and simmer for 5 minutes. Stir in the cucumber, five-spice powder, soy sauce, noodles, sliced roast pork, and bean sprouts. Cook another 2 minutes, then ladle into large bowls. Garnish with the fried onion flakes and coriander sprigs.

SERVES 4 (6–8 IF SHARING SEVERAL DISHES)

Indonesian prawn & noodle soup

150 g dried rice vermicelli

225 g fresh bean sprouts

1¼ cups vegetable oil

2 dried red chillies, deseeded

½ cup shelled peanuts

500 g fresh prawns, in their shells

6 cups water

1 teaspoon minced garlic

2 teaspoons minced lemongrass

1 teaspoon minced fresh ginger

2 tablespoons kecap manis (sweet soy sauce)

2 tablespoons tamarind concentrate (or lemon juice)

1 tablespoon soft brown sugar

Soak the vermicelli in hot water for 7 minutes, then drain. Blanch the bean sprouts in simmering water for 40 seconds, refresh in cold water, and drain.

Heat the oil over high heat until smoking, then reduce the heat to medium. Fry the chillies until crisp and well browned, remove from the oil and drain on a paper towel. Add the peanuts to the oil and fry to golden, then remove and cool. Chop finely and set aside.

Place the prawns in a saucepan with the water, garlic, lemongrass and ginger. Bring to the boil and simmer for 6 minutes. Lift out the prawns with a slotted spoon, set aside to cool for a few minutes, then remove the heads and shells and return these to the stock. Simmer for a further 10 minutes. Strain the broth into another pan and season with the kecap manis, tamarind and sugar. **>**

Slice each prawn in half lengthways. Distribute the noodles, bean sprouts, and prawns evenly among serving bowls and pour broth over. Crush the fried chillies and sprinkle, with the peanuts, over each bowl of soup.

SERVES 4–6

Pork & peas in rice vermicelli soup

350 g lean pork mince

1 tablespoon light soy sauce

1 teaspoon dark soy sauce

⅓ teaspoon minced garlic

2 teaspoons rice wine or
   dry sherry

1½ cups frozen green peas

150 g rice vermicelli

1½ tablespoons vegetable oil

1 tablespoon finely shredded
   fresh ginger

6½ cups pork stock

salt and white pepper

½ teaspoon sesame oil (optional)

⅓ cup sliced spring-onion
   greens

Place pork in a dish with the soy sauces, garlic and rice wine or sherry.
Mix well and set aside for 1 hour (refrigerate in warm weather).

Meanwhile, cook peas in lightly salted water until tender, and drain.
Soften the vermicelli in hot water for about 8 minutes, then drain and place
a bundle in each serving bowl. Heat the oil in a wok or frying-pan over high
heat and stir-fry the pork until lightly browned (about 4 minutes). Spoon
pork over the vermicelli, and add the peas and ginger.

Bring the stock to the boil and season to taste with salt and pepper. Add
the sesame oil, if using, then pour carefully into the bowls. Add spring-
onion greens just before serving.

SERVES 6

Laksa lemak

200 g green (raw) prawns, shelled and deveined

175 g frozen squid balls, halved

200 g dried rice vermicelli

175 g fresh bean sprouts

1 small cucumber

2 fresh chillies, deseeded

3 fresh kaffir lime leaves (optional)

SAUCE

5 dried red chillies

1 tablespoon coriander seeds

1 teaspoon cumin seeds

1 tablespoon chopped macadamia nuts

1 teaspoon ground turmeric

2 teaspoons shrimp paste

6 slices fresh ginger

4 slices galangal (optional)

1 stem lemongrass, chopped

1 tablespoon chopped fresh coriander (include the roots)

3 tablespoons vegetable oil

2 cups thin coconut milk

1 cup thick coconut milk

salt, pepper to taste and sugar

To make the sauce, first toast the chillies, coriander and cumin seeds in a dry pan over medium heat until they are very aromatic (about 2 minutes). Pour into a spice grinder and grind to a fine powder. Add the nuts and turmeric, and grind again. Toast the shrimp paste, or fry it in a little vegetable oil over medium heat for 40 seconds. >

Add the shrimp paste, ginger, galangal, lemongrass and fresh coriander to the spices and grind to a paste, adding a little of the oil if needed to prevent the blades clogging. Heat the oil in a medium-sized, heavy pan and gently fry this paste for about 4 minutes over medium heat until it is very aromatic. Add the thin coconut milk and bring to the boil, stirring.

Reduce the heat and simmer, partially covered, for about 12 minutes, then pour in the thick coconut milk. Check seasonings, adding salt, pepper and a little sugar to taste. Add the prawns and squid balls to the sauce and cook for 5–6 minutes. Meanwhile, blanch the vermicelli in boiling water for 30 seconds, drain, and blanch again. Drain thoroughly.

Divide the vermicelli between four deep bowls. Blanch the bean sprouts in boiling water, and drain. Cut the (unpeeled) cucumber in half, scoop out the seeds, and cut across into thin slices. Place the cucumber and bean sprouts on the noodles and pour the sauce over, distributing the prawns and squid balls evenly.

Add a little of the chopped chilli to each bowl and scatter the shredded lime leaves over the top. Serve the remaining chillies in a small dish.

SERVES 4

Sweet–sour noodle soup

225 g lean, boneless pork

625 g fresh rice-stick noodles
(or 375 g dried)

8 cloves garlic, peeled and
thinly sliced

½ cup vegetable oil

175 g Chinese cabbage

175 g cleaned squid

175 g fish balls, fresh (page 48)
or frozen

175 g small prawns, shelled
and deveined

1 tomato, peeled, deseeded
and diced

salt and white pepper

½ cup diced fresh pineapple

fish sauce and pickled chillies,
to serve

BROTH

2½ tablespoons tomato ketchup

3 tablespoons fish sauce

1½ tablespoons white vinegar

2 fresh green chillies, deseeded
and finely chopped

4 slices fresh ginger,
finely shredded

Place pork in a saucepan with 2 litres of water. Bring to the boil and simmer for about 45 minutes, until tender. Strain the cooking liquid into another saucepan and set aside. Place the pork on a plate to cool, then cut into thin slices.

Cover the fresh noodles with hot water for 3 minutes, then drain and set aside. (Soften dried noodles in boiling water, then drain.) **>**

Heat the oil in a small pan over medium–high heat and fry the garlic until browned, taking care it does not burn and therefore turn bitter. Remove to a paper towel to drain; reserve the oil for another recipe (it will add a wonderful nutty, garlicky taste).

Slice the cabbage finely, cut the squid into rings, and halve the fish balls. Bring the strained pork liquid to the boil, adding the broth ingredients. Simmer for 5–6 minutes, then season to taste with salt and pepper. Add the cabbage, seafood and tomato, and cook for about 5 minutes.

Drain the noodles and divide among soup bowls, adding pineapple and sliced pork to each. Pour the hot broth over and scatter with the fried garlic, adding some of the oil in which it cooked if you like a distinct garlic flavour.

Serve with extra fish sauce and pickled chillies on the side.

SERVES 4 (6–8 IF SHARING SEVERAL DISHES)

Prawns in coconut soup
with rice vermicelli

150 g dried rice vermicelli

450 g medium-sized green (raw)
 prawns, peeled and deveined
 but tails left on

1 large onion

2 tablespoons vegetable oil

3 teaspoons minced fresh ginger

½ teaspoon minced garlic

1 stem lemongrass, thinly sliced

3 cups coconut milk

2 teaspoons ground coriander

½ teaspoon shrimp paste

2½ tablespoons fish sauce

1 fresh red chilli, deseeded
 and chopped

salt and freshly ground
 black pepper

2½ cups water

2 tablespoons chopped fresh
 coriander leaves (or 2 fresh
 kaffir lime leaves, trimmed
 and very finely shredded)

Soak the vermicelli in warm water for 3 minutes; drain well. Rinse prawns
and dry with paper towels. Peel, halve and slice the onion thinly. Heat the
oil in a saucepan over medium–high heat and sauté the onion until golden.
Remove and reserve half of the onion, and continue cooking the remainder
until very well browned (about 6 minutes).

Add the ginger, garlic, lemongrass, coconut milk, ground coriander, and
shrimp paste to the pan. Cook over low heat for 20–25 minutes until the
sauce is well reduced, with a film of oil floating on the surface. Remove
half the sauce to a bowl and set aside. >

Add the reserved cooked onion, the fish sauce, chilli, salt, pepper and water to the sauce remaining in the pan, and bring to the boil. Reduce the heat and simmer for 20 minutes. Add the prawns and noodles and cook over medium heat until prawns are tender (about 3 minutes).

To serve, pour a portion of the vermicelli, prawns and sauce into each bowl. Spoon the reserved coconut sauce over, and garnish with the coriander or lime leaves. You may like to offer freshly squeezed lime juice, plus fish sauce, for guests to add at the table to their taste.

If lemongrass is to be used sliced, it must be cut very fine or its hard, wooden texture will spoil the dish. Hold it firmly on a cutting board and use a cleaver or very sharp paring knife to cut across the stem into paper-thin slices. It can be frozen in a small container.

SERVES 4 (6–8 IF SHARING SEVERAL DISHES)

Bean-thread vermicelli & chicken mousse in clear mushroom soup

12–18 dried shiitake mushrooms, soaked for 15 minutes in cold water and drained

1 kg skinless, boneless chicken pieces

2 spring onions, whites and green tops separated

6 thick slices fresh ginger

50 g bean-thread vermicelli

100 g skinless chicken breast fillet

2 egg whites

1 tablespoon minced spring onion (white parts only)

1 teaspoon soy sauce

⅓ teaspoon salt

2½ tablespoons cold water

12 snow pea shoots or spinach leaves

light soy sauce, and salt, to serve

Place mushrooms in a saucepan with 2.5 litres water, the chicken pieces, the spring-onion whites and the ginger. Bring to boil, reduce heat to low, and cook very slowly for 30 minutes, skimming from time to time. When done, strain and discard chicken parts, spring onions and ginger.

Bring a small pan of water to the boil, add the vermicelli, stir three times and then drain in a colander. Finely slice the spring-onion greens diagonally and set aside for garnish.

Cube the chicken breast, place in a food processor with the egg whites, minced spring-onion whites, salt and cold water, and grind to a smooth paste. Place mixture in a piping bag. ❯

Trim the stems from the mushrooms and return the caps to the broth with the drained vermicelli. Reheat to boiling, then pipe small sausages of the chicken mousse into the soup. Add the pea shoots or spinach leaves, and season to taste with soy sauce and salt. Heat for 2 minutes. Serve in bowls or a tureen.

SERVES 6–8

Chicken noodles in coconut soup

225 g skinless chicken breast fillet, cut into 1-cm cubes

2 teaspoons fish sauce

1 teaspoon rice wine or dry sherry

6 thin slices fresh ginger, finely shredded

1½ cups coconut milk

3 fresh or frozen kaffir lime leaves

1 stem lemongrass, halved lengthways

1 teaspoon salt

⅓ teaspoon white pepper

1 litre chicken stock

1 large tomato, cut into wedges

100 g fine rice vermicelli

extra fish sauce, and wedges of fresh lime, to serve

Place the chicken in a dish with the fish sauce, rice wine and ginger, and mix well. Cover with plastic wrap and set aside for 20 minutes.

Pour coconut milk into a medium-sized pan with a heavy base and bring almost to the boil over medium–high heat. Add the lime leaves, lemongrass, salt and pepper. Reduce the heat and simmer for 10 minutes, to reduce the liquid and intensify the flavour, stirring occasionally. Add chicken to pan and cook gently for 5 minutes, then add the stock and tomato, and bring barely to the boil. Add the vermicelli and cook until soft (1 minute). Serve in deep bowls, with fish sauce and lime wedges on the side.

SERVES 4–6

Hokkien mee soup

450 g stewing beef (round or
　　skirt) cut into 5-cm cubes

2½ tablespoons vegetable oil

225 g fresh hokkien noodles

100 g firm tofu

1½ teaspoons minced garlic

1 stalk celery, thinly sliced
　　diagonally

1 fresh red chilli

100 g green (raw) prawns,
　　shelled

175 g fish balls, fresh (page 48)
　　or frozen

½ cup diagonally sliced
　　spring-onion greens

75 g spinach leaves

salt and white pepper

light soy sauce

Brown beef in a heavy pan with half the vegetable oil, over high heat.
Add 2 litres water, bring to boil and simmer, partially covered, until meat
is tender (about 1 hour). Strain the stock (there should be about 6½ cups)
and keep hot. Cut the beef into smaller pieces.

Bring 1.5 litres water to the boil, add the noodles and cook for about
2 minutes, then drain. Divide the noodles between six soup bowls and
top with the beef pieces.

Cut the tofu into thin slices, stack the slices and cut into narrow strips.
In a small pan heat the remaining oil over medium–high heat. Stir-fry the

garlic, tofu, celery and chilli for 2½ minutes. Add the prawns and fish balls, and cook a further 1½ minutes, until the prawns turn pink. Pour on the hot stock, add the spring-onion greens and the spinach, and heat through. Add salt and pepper to taste, pour over the noodles, and serve with soy sauce.

The stock can be made ahead of time and refrigerated or frozen until needed. The remaining ingredients will take just a few minutes to prepare.

SERVES 6

Seafood noodles

Noodles are a perfect foil for succulent seafood, a marriage of simplicity and luxury.

From tender, snow-white rice ribbons through clear-as-glass bean threads to crisp-fried and crunchy vermicelli, noodles highlight the rich natural flavour of fish, prawns, crab and seafood of every kind. Try yellow hokkien noodles replete with dried and fresh prawns, egg noodles in hot and tangy bean sauces that showcase plump pink prawns, and tender squid and carved vegetables wok-tossed through soft Chinese egg noodles.

As with any seafood dishes, of course, the cardinal rules here are to buy the freshest seafood possible and to take care not to overcook it.

< Shanghai prawns in tomato sauce
on wheat noodles (page 78)

Shanghai prawns in tomato sauce on wheat noodles

250 g green (raw) prawns, shelled and deveined

2 teaspoons fish sauce

2 teaspoons cornflour

2 spring onions

1 medium-sized onion

1 stalk celery

175 g thin wheat noodles (e.g. somen)

2½ tablespoons vegetable oil

1½ tablespoons very finely shredded fresh ginger

1 tablespoon light soy sauce

½ cup chicken stock

3 tablespoons tomato ketchup

2 teaspoons rice or cider vinegar

1 teaspoon sriracha (Thai hot chilli sauce)

½ teaspoon sugar

½ teaspoon sesame oil

freshly ground black pepper

2 teaspoons cornflour

Make a deep cut in each prawn along the centre of its back, so it will curl during cooking. Rinse, drain, and dry on paper towels. Mix with the fish sauce and cornflour, and set aside for 10 minutes.

Trim the spring onions, cut the white parts into 2-cm pieces, and slice the green tops for garnish. Set aside. Peel the onion and cut into narrow wedges. Cut the celery into thin diagonal slices. Combine the sauce ingredients in a bowl. Bring 1.5 litres of water to the boil, add the noodles and cook for just a few minutes, until tender, then drain.

Heat half the oil in a wok or large frying-pan over medium–high heat. Stir-fry the prawns with half the ginger until the prawns curl and turn pink, then remove them and set aside. Add to the pan the white parts of the spring onions, plus the celery and onion, and stir-fry over medium–high heat until softened but not browned. Sizzle the soy sauce over and cook briefly, then remove all the ingredients to a plate and set aside.

Heat the remaining oil in the wok over high heat. Stir-fry the noodles for 1 minute, then spread on a serving plate. Rinse out the wok and reheat over medium–high heat. Stir the sauce, pour into the wok and stir until boiling, then lower the heat and simmer for 1½ minutes. Add the cooked spring onions, celery and onion, and heat through for 1 minute, then add the prawns and heat briefly, mixing well. Pour contents of the wok over the noodles, garnish with the spring-onion greens and ginger, and serve at once.

SERVES 2–3 (4–5 IF SHARING SEVERAL DISHES)

Seafood rice ribbons

675 g fresh rice ribbon noodles

425 g fresh seafood (scallops, prawns, squid, crab meat, white fish)

2 teaspoons minced fresh ginger

1½ tablespoons light soy sauce

¾ teaspoon salt

3 spring onions

12 small spinach leaves

2½ tablespoons vegetable oil

1 fresh red chilli, deseeded and sliced

2 tablespoons chopped fresh coriander

SAUCE

¾ cup chicken stock

1 teaspoon cornflour

salt and white pepper

Bring 2.5 litres of water to the boil, add the noodles and immediately pour into a colander to drain. Cover with cold water, and set aside.

Cut seafood into bite-sized pieces. Place in a dish with the ginger, soy sauce and salt, and mix well. Set aside for 20 minutes.

Trim the spring onions, cut white parts in half lengthways and then into 2.5-cm pieces. Shred some of the green tops for garnish. Combine the sauce ingredients in a bowl. Blanch the spinach in a small pan of boiling water for 30 seconds and drain.

Heat half the oil in a wok or frying-pan over high heat. Stir-fry the seafood until it changes colour. Add the spring onions, stir-fry for 40 seconds and ❯

then add the seasoned seafood and stir-fry for 1½ minutes or until cooked. Remove to a plate.

Drain the noodles thoroughly. Rinse and dry the wok, add the remaining oil, and reheat. Stir-fry the noodles until each strand is glazed with the oil. Stir the prepared sauce and pour over the noodles, cook for 1½ minutes, then return the seafood and add the chilli and spinach leaves. Stir-fry for 1 minute more, and season to taste with salt and pepper. Arrange on a platter, and garnish with the coriander and spring-onion greens.

SERVES 3–4 (6 IF SHARING SEVERAL DISHES)

Sweet & sour seafood on a cloud

6 cups vegetable oil for
   deep-frying

65 g rice vermicelli

150 g white fish

⅓ cup sliced scallops

⅓ cup sliced squid hoods

6 medium-sized prawns, shelled
   and deveined

cornflour for coating

1 stalk celery, thinly sliced
   diagonally

⅓ cup sliced bamboo shoots

1 small onion, cut into
   narrow wedges

1 small carrot, thinly sliced
   diagonally

SAUCE

¾ cup chicken stock

½ cup sugar

⅓ cup rice vinegar

2 teaspoons shredded
   fresh ginger

½ teaspoon chopped garlic

3 tablespoons tomato ketchup

1 tablespoon cornflour

½ teaspoon salt

⅓ teaspoon sesame oil

red food colouring (optional)

First, combine the sauce ingredients in a bowl and set aside.

In a deep-fryer or wok, heat the oil over medium–high heat to 190°C.
Add the vermicelli in a single piece: it should expand into a puffy white >

cloud within seconds. Turn to cook the other side, making sure the whole portion has been exposed to the oil and is therefore crisp and white. Lift onto a rack over a double thickness of paper towel to drain. Set aside.

Cut the fish into thin slices, then into 3-cm squares. Halve the scallops horizontally. Cut the squid into 3.5-cm squares and use a sharp knife to score the inside surface in a criss-cross pattern. Bring a pan of water to the boil, add the squid pieces and blanch for 15 seconds (they will curl into 'flowers'), then drain and set aside. If preferred, simply cut the squid tubes into rings.

Coat all the seafood very lightly with cornflour. Pour off all but ½ cup of the oil from the pan in which you cooked the vermicelli, and reserve for another use. Reheat over high heat until a haze of smoke floats over the pan. Stir-fry the seafood for 2 minutes until firm, then remove and set aside. Discard this oil and add another 1½ tablespoons of the deep-frying oil to the pan. Reheat over medium heat and stir-fry the celery, bamboo shoots, onion and carrot for about 1½ minutes. Stir the prepared sauce, pour into the pan, and bring to the boil. Cook, stirring often, for 2–3 minutes.

Return seafood to the pan and heat gently for 2 minutes. Place the noodles on a serving platter and crush lightly with the back of a spatula. Ladle the sauce over the noodles, and serve.

SERVES 2 (MORE IF SHARING SEVERAL DISHES)

Little prawn & noodle parcels

100 g dried thin rice-stick
    noodles

175 g boiled or roasted pork

175 g cooked, shelled prawns

4 spring onions, trimmed and
    diagonally sliced

⅓ cup fresh coriander leaves

⅓ cup mixed mint leaves
    (spearmint, Vietnamese, etc.)

⅓ cup shredded carrot

12 butter lettuce leaves

extra spring-onion greens for
    tying parcels (optional)

nuoc cham (Vietnamese sauce:
    page 235)

Soak noodles in boiling water to soften; drain well. Cut the pork into julienne strips and cut the prawns lengthways.

Arrange all the ingredients attractively on a platter for your guests to make their own parcels, wrapping a little of each ingredient in a piece of lettuce leaf. Alternatively, you can prepare parcels beforehand (trim the edges neatly), tying with a strip of spring-onion green.

Serve the sauce in bowls, for dipping.

SERVES 4–6

Steamed fish with bean threads

500 g white fish fillets, cut into
2.5-cm pieces

2½ tablespoons fish sauce

75 g dried bean-thread
vermicelli

6 dried black mushrooms,
soaked for 25 minutes in
warm water

1–2 teaspoon vegetable oil

1 small carrot, peeled and
julienned

¼ cup sliced bamboo shoots,
julienned

¼ cup peeled and seeded
cucumber, julienned

½ stalk celery, julienned

3 slices fresh ginger,
finely shredded

2 spring onions, trimmed,
cut into 5-cm lengths and
shredded lengthways

⅓ teaspoon black pepper

4 tablespoons thick
coconut milk

6 sprigs fresh coriander

Sprinkle the fish with 1 tablespoon of the fish sauce and set aside. Place
the noodles in a dish, pour boiling water over, and soak for 30 seconds.
Drain and then cut into 5-cm lengths with kitchen shears.

Drain the mushrooms, squeeze out excess water, trim off the stems, and
shred the caps finely. Brush the bottom of a heatproof dish with oil. Mix
the noodles with prepared vegetables (use only half the spring onions, and
reserve the rest for garnish) and arrange half in the dish. **>**

Place the fish on top in a single layer, sprinkle with pepper, and cover with the remaining vegetables and noodles. Pour the remaining fish sauce evenly over the dish.

Select a steamer or pan large enough to accommodate the dish. Pour in 5 cm of hot water and position a rack in the pan to hold the dish. Set dish on the rack, place over medium–high heat, cover, and steam for 10 minutes. Pour on the coconut milk and steam for a further 6–7 minutes. Garnish with the coriander and the reserved spring onion, and serve in the dish.

SERVES 4 (6–8 IF SHARING SEVERAL DISHES)

Miso soba

325 g dried soba noodles

100 g kamaboko (Japanese fish cake)

4 medium-sized prawns, peeled and deveined

1 teaspoon dried wakame (curly seaweed), soaked in cold water for 25 minutes

7 cups ichiban dashi (page 18)

1¾ tablespoons white miso (soybean paste)

3 tablespoons finely sliced spring onions rinsed

4 strips lemon peel

Bring 2 litres of water to the boil, add the noodles and return water to the boil. Add 1 cup of cold water, bring again to the boil, then add ½ cup cold water. When it has boiled again, add another ½ cup of cold water, then cook the noodles until barely tender. Drain, rinse with cold water, then transfer to a wire strainer and set aside.

Cut the fish cake into 8 slices. Butterfly each prawn, make an incision through the centre, insert the tail and pull through to the other side. Bring a small pan of water to a boil, add the prawns and cook until they turn pink (about 1 minute). Remove with a slotted spoon.

Drain the wakame and cut into small strips. Pour the stock into a pot, add the seaweed, and bring to the boil. Remove from heat and stir in the miso (do not let stock boil again after this point).   >

Plunge strainer of noodles into a pan of boiling water, or pour boiling water over, to reheat. Divide between four bowls.

Pour the stock over the noodles, add 1 prawn and 2 slices of fish cake to each bowl, plus some of the wakame, a sprinkle of sliced spring onions and a strip of lemon peel. Serve.

Japanese cooks add sliced spring onions to many dishes, for flavour or as a garnish, but they do not appreciate an excessively oniony taste. To eliminate this, the slices are placed in a clean cloth, rinsed thoroughly and the cloth is then squeezed until all excess liquid has been removed. This leaves a very mild onion flavour.

SERVES 4

Tempura soba

450 g dried soba noodles

8 large prawns, shelled
and deveined

½ cup plain flour

3 cups vegetable oil for
deep-frying

2 tablespoons sesame oil

6 cups Japanese noodle broth
(page 19)

50 g thinly sliced bamboo shoots

2 tablespoons finely sliced
spring onions, rinsed
(see note page 91)

⅓ sheet nori (compressed
seaweed), shredded

1½ teaspoons shichimi
(Japanese pepper condiment)
or toasted white sesame seeds

4 strips lemon peel (optional)

BATTER

1 egg yolk

1 cup iced water

1 cup plain flour, sifted

Bring 2 litres of water to the boil, add the noodles, and bring back to the
boil. Pour in ½ cup of cold water, return to the boil, add another ½ cup of
cold water, return again to the boil, then add another ½ cup of cold water
and cook until the noodles are tender. Drain

Coat the prawns lightly and evenly with the ½ cup flour, shaking off excess.

Heat the deep-frying oil to 190°C, then add the sesame oil. Meanwhile,
heat the broth to boiling, then lower heat and keep warm.

To prepare the batter, beat the egg yolk into the iced water. Place flour in a bowl, add the egg mix and stir just a few times with chopsticks (overmixing ruins tempura batter). Dip the prawns in, one by one, coating generously. Deep-fry the prawns until batter is crisp and golden, and prawns are barely cooked through (about 1¼ minutes). Lift out, drain on paper towels, and set aside.

Divide the noodles between four deep bowls. Pour in the broth, add the bamboo shoots and spring onions, sprinkle with the shichimi or the sesame seeds, and the nori, and add a strip of lemon peel if desired. Place 2 prawns on top, and serve at once.

SERVES 4

Seafood noodle balls

175 g dried thin egg noodles

325 g seafood (e.g. prawns, crab meat, scallops, mussels)

2 spring onions

4 thin slices fresh ginger

8 canned water chestnuts, drained

1 cup loosely packed fresh coriander leaves

⅔ teaspoon salt

⅓ teaspoon white pepper

pinch of ground chilli

1 egg white, lightly beaten

2 cups vegetable oil, for deep-frying

2 tablespoons sesame oil

sweet chilli sauce

Bring 1 litre of lightly salted water to a boil, add the noodles, and cook for about 3½ minutes, until tender. Drain and set aside.

If using prawns, shell and devein them. Slice the spring-onion greens finely on the diagonal and set aside for garnish. Chop the white parts roughly, place in a food processor with the ginger, water chestnuts and coriander, and grind for a few seconds. Add the seafood and process to a smooth paste, adding the salt, pepper, chilli and egg white. Sprinkle with 2 tablespoons iced water and process until the mixture is very smooth and voluminous (about 45 seconds).

Cut the well-drained noodles into 2.5-cm pieces. With wet hands, form the seafood paste into small balls and roll in the noodles, coating evenly. **>**

Heat the vegetable oil to 190°C in a wok or large frying-pan, then add the sesame oil. Fry the seafood balls until golden–brown and cooked through (about 3 minutes), turning occasionally. Retrieve with a wire skimmer and drain briefly on a double thickness of paper towel.

To serve, arrange the seafood balls on a platter lined with a paper napkin or lettuce leaves, and insert a toothpick in each one. Scatter with the spring-onion greens, and serve hot.

MAKES ABOUT 20

Corn & crab with Japanese noodles

325 g dried ramen or udon
noodles

100 g roasted pork fillet,
thinly sliced

225 g corn kernels (fresh,
frozen or canned)

4 blue swimmer crab claws
boiled in lightly salted water
for 6 minutes

1½ tablespoons sliced spring-
onion greens, rinsed
(see note page 91)

BROTH

2 litres ichiban dashi
(page 18)

10 g dried wakame (curly
seaweed), soaked for 25
minutes in warm water

1½–2 tablespoons white miso
(soybean paste)

2 teaspoons caster sugar
(optional)

Bring 2 litres of water to the boil and add the noodles. Simmer for about
3 minutes, until tender, then drain.

To make the broth, bring the dashi to a boil with the wakame and simmer for
5 minutes. Retrieve the wakame with a slotted spoon and cut into shreds.
Remove broth from the heat and stir in the miso and sugar (if using).

Divide the noodles between four deep bowls. To each add a portion of corn,
some wakame, several slices of pork, a crab claw, and a sprinkling of
spring-onion greens. Pour the broth over, and serve at once.

SERVES 4

Prickly prawns

18 medium-sized green (raw) prawns, shelled
  (leave the tail intact) and deveined
about 1 cup cornflour
3 large egg whites
175 g dried rice vermicelli
5 cups vegetable oil, for deep-frying
sweet or hot chilli sauce

Coat the prawns lightly with ¾ cup of the cornflour. Beat egg whites to soft
peaks and fold in 3 tablespoons cornflour. Place the vermicelli in a strong
plastic or paper bag and crush with a rolling pin into pieces about 2 cm
long. Pour onto a plate or tray.

Heat the oil in a wok or deep pan to 190°C, then reduce heat slightly. Dip
each prawn into the egg-white batter, covering thickly, and coat evenly with
the crushed vermicelli.

Slide three prawns into the oil and fry for about 2 minutes, until golden.
Turn several times, using a wire skimmer and taking care not to break
the vermicelli. Remove to absorbent paper to drain. Repeat with the
remaining prawns.

To serve as a cocktail snack, arrange prawns on a platter lined with a paper napkin or lettuce leaves, and serve with a small bowl of chilli sauce for dipping. As a first course, present on wide plates, surrounded by mixed salad greens and herbs sprinkled with a well-flavoured, balsamic vinegar-based vinaigrette.

MAKES 18

Spicy prawns in a tangle of noodles

125 g dried egg noodles

4 shiitake mushrooms
(if dried, soak for 25 minutes
in warm water)

1 medium-sized carrot, peeled
and julienned

4 large snow peas, julienned

1 leek, trimmed and julienned

12 medium–large green (raw)
prawns, shelled (leave tail
intact) and deveined

1 tablespoon olive oil

3 tablespoons chopped
spring onions

¼ cup diced unripe mango
(or substitute cucumber)

¼ cup deseeded and diced
tomato

2 tablespoons chopped fresh
coriander leaves

BEAN-SAUCE DRESSING

1 teaspoon yellow bean sauce

1 teaspoon chilli-bean paste

⅓ cup light soy sauce

2 teaspoons sugar

2 tablespoons rice vinegar

⅓ cup olive oil

few drops chilli oil or Tabasco

To make the bean-sauce dressing, simply combine all the ingredients
in a bowl.

Bring 1 litre of water to the boil, salt lightly, and add the noodles. Cook till
tender, drain, and cool under running cold water. Set aside to drain again. >

Drain soaked mushrooms (if using) and squeeze out excess water. Remove mushroom stems and shred the caps finely. Place the mushrooms, carrot, snow peas and leeks on top of the noodles.

Heat the oil in a wok or frying-pan over high heat and sauté the prawns until they change colour. Add 1 tablespoon of the dressing and sauté until prawns are cooked and glazed with the sauce. Remove from the pan. Add the spring onions, mango and tomato to the pan and sauté briefly. Return the prawns and mix. Keep warm.

Pour boiling water over the noodles and vegetables to reheat, then drain thoroughly. Transfer to a bowl, pour the dressing over, and toss until well mixed. Arrange the noodles in mounds on each plate, with the prawns on top. Scatter with the coriander leaves and serve at once.

SERVES 4 AS AN APPETISER

Warm noodles with crab & abalone

2 tablespoons fresh or frozen
    green peas (or sliced beans)

1 stalk celery

½ cup cooked crab meat

1 abalone, canned or cooked

150 g dried thin egg noodles

½ tomato, peeled, deseeded
    and diced

4 lettuce leaves

DRESSING

1 tablespoon sesame oil

½ cup chicken stock

½ teaspoon salt

½ teaspoon tahini

½ teaspoon chilli oil

½ teaspoon light soy sauce

½ teaspoon Chinese red vinegar

Parboil the peas or beans until barely tender. Dice celery, parboil for
1 minute, and drain.

Separate the crab meat into small pieces. Cut the abalone into small dice.
Bring 1.5 litres of lightly salted water to the boil, add the noodles, cook for
about 4 minutes until al dente, and drain. Combine the dressing ingredients,
pour over the noodles, and set aside for 5–6 minutes.

Add the prepared peas or beans, celery, tomato and seafood to the
noodles, toss to combine, and arrange over the lettuce on a serving plate.

SERVES 4

Noodles with poultry

There's far more to chicken and noodles than comforting, restorative soup. Dishes like Quail Wearing Pearls in Noodle Baskets and Thai Chicken on Spicy Rice Noodles (Gai Pad Thai) evoke exotic places and suggest stimulating flavours.

Slivers, slices and shreds of chicken nestle companionably amidst tangles of noodles. Teamed with creamy crab meat, pungent garlic chives, or shreds of fresh ginger they create simple, satisfying meals in minutes. Turkey, duck and quail lend imposing flavours to noodle dishes, too, and are often teamed with boldly flavoured sauces based on sesame, soy and hoisin.

< Spicy Thai chicken on crisp noodles (page 106)

Spicy Thai chicken on crisp noodles

400 g skinless chicken breast
    fillets

1 tablespoon Thai red
    curry paste

1 large onion, finely sliced

1½ tablespoons peanut oil

4 × ¼ capsicums (red, green,
    gold, yellow), deseeded and
    julienned

½ cup coconut milk

1.5 litres vegetable oil, for
    deep-frying

100 g dried rice vermicelli

chopped, roasted peanuts
    for garnish

Cut the chicken into 1.5-cm strips and place in a dish. Brush with
2 teaspoons of the curry paste, and set aside for 40 minutes.

In a small frying-pan, sauté the onion in the peanut oil over medium–high
heat, until golden. Add the peppers and cook for about 1½ minutes, to
soften. Remove and set aside.

Reheat the pan and sauté the chicken strips for about 2½ minutes, until
cooked through, then remove from the pan. Pour coconut milk into pan and
add the remaining curry paste. Simmer for 4–5 minutes over medium heat.
Return the chicken, onion and peppers to pan, heat through and then keep
warm over very low heat.

In a deep pan or wok, heat the vegetable oil to 190°C. Add the vermicelli in a bundle and flip it as soon as it has expanded and turned fluffy and white. Cook the other side only very briefly. When fully expanded, remove from the oil to drain on a double layer of paper towel.

Transfer drained vermicelli to a serving plate and press with a spatula to partially crumble it, or crumble and serve on individual plates with the chicken and vegetables nestled in the centre.

SERVES 4–6 AS AN APPETISER (2 AS A MAIN COURSE)

Chicken & garlic chives on fried noodles

150 g dried thin egg noodles

¼ cup vegetable oil

175 g skinless chicken breast fillet

2 teaspoons light soy sauce

1 teaspoon rice wine or dry sherry

1½ teaspoons cornflour

1 tablespoon shredded fresh ginger

12 garlic chives, cut into 2.5-cm lengths

salt and white pepper

oyster sauce

SAUCE

¾ cup chicken stock

2 teaspoons light soy sauce

⅓ teaspoon sugar

3 teaspoons cornflour

Bring 1.5 litres of water to the boil. Add the noodles and 1 tablespoon of the vegetable oil. Return to boil, reduce the heat so the water is barely bubbling, then stir the noodles to untangle them and cook for 3¼ minutes. Drain well and spread on a large plate to partially dry.

Slice the chicken thinly and cut into fine strips. Combine the soy sauce, rice wine or sherry, and cornflour in a bowl, add the chicken, and mix well. Set aside for 15 minutes. Meanwhile, combine the sauce ingredients in a bowl and set aside. **>**

Heat 2½ tablespoons of the vegetable oil in a wok or pan over medium–high heat. Spread the noodles in an even layer in the pan and cook until the underside and the outer edge are crisp. Turn in one piece and cook the other side, then lift onto a serving plate.

Add the remaining oil, if needed, and reheat the pan over high heat. Stir-fry the chicken until it turns white (about 40 seconds), then add the ginger and garlic chives and stir-fry for 30 seconds, mixing with the chicken. Stir the prepared sauce, pour into the pan and cook, stirring continuously, until it thickens. Season with salt and pepper, and pour over the noodles.

Drizzle oyster sauce over the dish and serve at once.

SERVES 2 (4 IF SHARING SEVERAL DISHES)

Shanghai brown-sauce noodles

275 g fresh thick noodles

222 g Chinese cabbage

225 g chicken breast fillet,
   skin on

3 tablespoons vegetable oil

2 teaspoons grated fresh ginger

2 tablespoons dark soy sauce

2 tablespoons hoisin sauce

2 cups chicken stock

1 teaspoon sesame oil

white pepper

SEASONING FOR CHICKEN

1 tablespoon light soy sauce

1 teaspoon dark soy sauce

2 teaspoons rice wine or
   dry sherry

1 teaspoon cornflour

Bring 2.5 litres of water to the boil, add noodles, and cook for 1 minute. Drain, and spread on a tray to dry.

Finely shred the cabbage stems and cut the leaves into 2-cm slices. Cut the chicken into thin slices, then into shreds, place in a dish with the chicken seasoning ingredients, and set aside for 10 minutes.

Heat half the oil in a wok over high heat and stir-fry the chicken for 1½ minutes. Remove, add the cabbage and ginger, and stir-fry for 1 minute or until cabbage is wilted. Remove. ➤

Add remaining oil to the wok and stir-fry drained noodles for 2 minutes. Add the dark soy and hoisin sauces, and stir-fry for 1 minute. Pour in the stock and simmer for 5 minutes. Return the chicken and cabbage to the wok, stir to mix and heat through, tossing, for 2 minutes.

Transfer to a serving plate and sprinkle with sesame oil and white pepper.

Chinese cabbage keeps well, unwrapped, in the vegetable compartment of the refrigerator. If you have any left over from a recipe, use it up in stir-fries, or poach it until tender and serve with a sauce of flaked crab meat in chicken stock thickened with cornflour.

SERVES 2–4

Beijing noodle hot pot

175 g flat wheat noodles

⅔ cup chicken leg meat, diced

2 teaspoons rice wine or
    dry sherry

1 teaspoon ginger juice (see note
    page 49)

100 g fresh or frozen
    seafood balls

6 dried shiitake mushrooms,
    soaked for 25 minutes in
    ½ cup hot water

3 baby bok choy or other Asian
    greens, coarsely shredded

½ cup sliced straw mushrooms

⅓ cup sliced bamboo shoots

3 small tomatoes, quartered

2 spring onions, trimmed and
    cut into 5-cm lengths

225 g soft tofu, cubed

BROTH

6½ cups chicken stock

2 tablespoons light soy sauce

1½ teaspoons salt

¾ teaspoon sugar

Cook the noodles in boiling water until al dente, then drain. Pour into
a clay pot or a casserole, and set aside.

Place the chicken in a bowl, add the rice wine and ginger juice, mix well,
and leave for 10 minutes. Cut the seafood balls in half. Drain the shiitake
mushrooms, reserving the liquid, and remove stems. Cook cabbages in
boiling water until crisp-tender (about 2½ minutes), then drain.

Arrange chicken, seafood balls, vegetables and tofu over the noodles. Combine the broth ingredients in a saucepan, add reserved mushroom liquid and bring to boil. Pour into the casserole and simmer gently over medium heat for 10 minutes. Serve in the casserole.

To cut soft tofu into even-sized cubes that won't collapse, hold the block in the palm of your hand and gently cut downward with a knife that is not excessively sharp. Slide the cubes from your hand directly into the wok or pan.

SERVES 6–10 IF SHARING SEVERAL DISHES

Rice-stick noodles
with chicken & prawns

1 stem lemongrass

3 fresh green chillies, deseeded
   and sliced

¼ cup macadamia nuts or
   almonds

1 teaspoon ground turmeric

1 teaspoon minced garlic

1 teaspoon minced fresh ginger

3 tablespoons vegetable oil

800 g chicken pieces (with
   bones)

salt and freshly ground
   black pepper

½ cup sliced shallots

1½ tablespoons light soy sauce

2½ cups coconut milk

4 dried curry leaves or 1 bay leaf

350 g green (raw) prawns,
   shelled and deveined

675 g fresh rice-stick noodles
   (or 275 g dried)

GARNISH

3–4 sprigs basil

1 hard-boiled egg, sliced

1 tablespoon fried onion flakes
   (page 237)

Place the lemongrass, chillies, nuts, turmeric, garlic and ginger in a spice
grinder or blender, and grind to a paste. Heat 1 tablespoon of the oil in a
medium-sized, heavy-based saucepan over medium–high heat and fry
paste for about 2 minutes, stirring frequently.

Season chicken pieces with salt and pepper, add to the pan with the
shallots and fry over medium–high heat until chicken is lightly browned.
Add soy sauce, coconut milk, 1½ cups water, and the curry leaves, and   >

bring to the boil. Immediately reduce heat and simmer, partially covered, for about 45 minutes, until the chicken is tender. Add the prawns and cook for another 3 minutes. Season to taste with salt and pepper.

When the chicken is almost done, bring 2.5 litres of water to a boil and salt sparingly. Add the noodles and cook for 40 seconds, then drain immediately. (If using dried noodles, cook for about 3¼ minutes, until tender, and drain.) Divide noodles between three or four deep bowls, or place in a tureen.

Remove chicken from sauce with a slotted spoon and place one or two pieces in each bowl, or debone and tear the meat into strips. Pour the sauce over and garnish with a sprig of basil, a slice or two of egg, and the onion flakes. Serve at once.

SERVES 3–4

Crispy Thai noodles (mee krob)

100 g skinless chicken breast
fillet

1 tablespoon fish sauce

1 cup peanut oil

75 g fresh firm tofu, diced

100 g small green (raw) prawns,
shelled and deveined

2 spring onions, trimmed
and chopped

2 cloves garlic, minced

extra 3–4 cups oil, for
deep-frying

200 g dried rice vermicelli

75 g fresh bean sprouts

6–8 garlic chives, cut into 5-cm
lengths

1 wok omelette (page 240)

SAUCE

½ cup white sugar

2 tablespoons fresh lime juice

1 tablespoon white vinegar

2 tablespoons fish sauce

2 tablespoons tomato ketchup

2 tablespoons water

1 teaspoon mild ground chilli

First prepare the sauce. Combine sauce ingredients in a small saucepan, bring to the boil, then reduce heat and simmer for 2 minutes, then remove and leave to cool.

Marinate the chicken in the fish sauce for 10 minutes. Meanwhile, heat the peanut oil in a large wok over high heat until a haze of smoke appears over the pan. Carefully add the diced tofu and fry, stirring occasionally, >

until golden–brown on the surface. Remove with a wire skimmer and set aside on absorbent paper to drain.

In the same oil, fry the chicken until it changes colour and is lightly cooked (about 1 minute). Remove and set aside. Carefully pour off all but 2 tablespoons of the oil, and reserve. Reheat the remaining oil and sauté the prawns, spring onions and garlic until the prawns turn pink, then remove and set aside with the chicken.

Rinse the wok and dry thoroughly. Pour in the deep-frying oil and heat over high heat to about 190°C. Place the vermicelli in a bag and bat with a rolling pin to break into short lengths. Pour half into the oil to cook for just a few seconds, turning the mass over with a wire skimmer as soon as it expands and turns snowy-white and removing it before it begins to colour. Cook the remaining vermicelli in the same way.

Pour off the oil and wipe out the wok. Pour in 2 tablespoons of the oil reserved from cooking the tofu and chicken, and reheat over high heat until smoky. Add half the cooked vermicelli and half the sauce, and turn quickly until each strand is coated and the sauce absorbed, then remove to a plate. Cook the remaining vermicelli and sauce in the same way, then return the first batch to the pan with the other cooked ingredients. Mix briskly.

To serve, mound into a cone shape on a serving plate. Garnish with the bean sprouts and garlic chives (and extra spring-onion pieces, if you like) and serve while still hot and crisp.

SERVES 4 (6–8 IF SHARING SEVERAL DISHES)

Fried noodles with chicken (gai pad thai)

275 g dried rice-stick noodles

4 tablespoons peanut or
vegetable oil

100 g firm tofu, diced

2 × wok omelettes (page 240)

225 g skinless chicken breast
fillet

3 shallots, sliced

1 teaspoon minced garlic

1 tablespoon dried shrimp,
finely chopped

⅓ cup coarsely chopped, roasted
unsalted peanuts

100 g fresh bean sprouts

3 spring onions, cut into
2.5-cm lengths

salt and white pepper

SAUCE

1½ cups water

1 tablespoon tamarind
concentrate

⅓ cup palm or dark-brown
sugar

2½ tablespoons fish sauce

ACCOMPANIMENTS

seeded and sliced fresh
red chillies

lime wedges

white sugar

garlic chives, cut into
5-cm lengths

roasted chilli flakes
(see note page 54)

extra fish sauce

Cover noodles with hot water and set aside to soften (about 15 minutes,
though time may vary for different brands). Drain in a colander. ❯

Combine sauce ingredients in a small saucepan and bring to the boil. Simmer until reduced to approximately ¾ cup, then set aside.

Heat the oil in a wok over high heat and fry the diced tofu until the surface is golden. Remove, set aside, and reserve the oil.

Cut chicken into 1-cm cubes. Return half the reserved oil to the wok and sauté chicken until it changes colour. Add shallots, garlic and dried shrimp, and sauté for about 1½ minutes. Remove.

Add remaining reserved oil to wok and reheat over high heat until oil is smoking. Drain the noodles, transfer to the wok and sauté briefly. Return the other sautéed ingredients to the wok and add the shredded omelette, the peanuts, bean sprouts and spring onions, plus salt and pepper to taste. Sauté for 1½ minutes, then pour in the sauce. Cook, stirring continuously, until ingredients are well mixed and sauce has been absorbed.

Transfer noodles to a large plate and surround with the prepared accompaniments (or serve them separately in small dishes).

SERVES 2–4 (UP TO 8 IF SHARING SEVERAL DISHES)

Spicy Thai chicken & tofu on rice sticks

275 g skinless chicken breast fillet

1 tablespoon fish sauce

150 g dried rice-stick noodles

4 spring onions, trimmed

4 snake beans, or 12 young green beans

2 teaspoons Thai red curry paste

1 cup thick coconut milk

1 × 2.5-cm piece lemongrass (the pale-green shoot end)

2 thin slices fresh ginger

⅓ cup peanut oil

salt and white pepper

50 g fried tofu cubes

Cut the chicken into 1-cm cubes and marinate with the fish sauce for 10 minutes. Bring 1.5 litres of lightly salted water to the boil, add the noodles and cook for about 5 minutes until tender. Drain, cover with cold water, and set aside.

Cut the white parts of the spring onions into 2.5-cm lengths, and slice the green tops thinly (reserve for garnish). Cut the beans into 2.5-cm lengths, cook in boiling water for 2 minutes, then drain.

Combine the curry paste and coconut milk in a saucepan. Bruise the lemongrass to release the flavour and add to the pan along with the ginger. Bring to the boil, then reduce heat and simmer for 15 minutes to thicken the sauce and intensify its flavours. >

Heat half the oil in a medium-sized saucepan, sauté the tofu cubes for 2 minutes, then remove and set aside. Reheat the pan, add the chicken and stir-fry until barely cooked (1½ minutes). Return tofu to pan, add the coconut sauce along with ½ cup water, and bring almost to the boil. Reduce heat and simmer for about 7 minutes. Check the seasonings, adding salt and pepper to taste.

Meanwhile, heat remaining oil in a wok or large frying-pan over high heat until smoking. Stir-fry the spring onions and beans briefly, then remove. Reheat the pan, add the well-drained noodles, and stir-fry for 2 minutes. Return the beans and spring onions, and mix in.

Spread wok contents on a serving platter or shallow dish. Pour the sauce over, garnish with the spring-onion greens, and serve.

Fried tofu cubes are available in packs of 6 or 12 at Asian food stores. Store in the refrigerator until ready to use; any unused portion should be tightly wrapped in plastic and returned to the refrigerator. If you need to make your own, purchase firm, fresh bean curd, cut into 2.5-cm cubes, and fry in deep oil over high heat until surface is a rich golden-brown.

SERVES 3–4 (4–6 IF SHARING SEVERAL DISHES)

Rice-stick noodles
with ginger & garlic chives

275 g skinless chicken breast
fillet

1 tablespoon fish sauce

1 teaspoon rice wine or
dry sherry

1 teaspoon cornflour

225 g dried rice-stick noodles
(or 550 g fresh rice ribbon
noodles)

3 tablespoons peanut or
vegetable oil

1 teaspoon minced fresh ginger

¾ teaspoon minced garlic

⅓ cup fresh bean sprouts

1½ tablespoons sliced
bamboo shoots

18 garlic chives, cut into
4-cm lengths

salt and white pepper

1 fresh red chilli, deseeded and
finely shredded

1 tablespoon chopped fresh
coriander

1 tablespoon crushed, unsalted
roasted peanuts

¼ teaspoon roasted chilli flakes
(see note page 54)

lime wedges and fish sauce,
to serve

SAUCE

⅓ cup chicken stock

2 tablespoons fish sauce

1 teaspoon cornflour

¼ teaspoon black pepper

1 teaspoon sugar

Slice the chicken thinly and cut into fine shreds. Combine the fish sauce,
rice wine and cornflour in a bowl, add the chicken and mix well. Set aside
to marinate for 20 minutes. ➤

Meanwhile, combine sauce ingredients in a bowl and set aside. Cook dried noodles in boiling water for 1½ minutes until barely tender, and drain well. (If using fresh noodles, cover with warm water for 20 seconds, then drain.)

Heat half the oil in a wok over high heat until smoking. Stir-fry the marinated chicken with the ginger and garlic for 2 minutes, then push to the side of the wok. Add bean sprouts, bamboo shoots and garlic chives to wok and stir-fry for 30 seconds. Mix the ingredients together, then remove from wok.

Heat remaining oil in the wok, stir-fry noodles over high heat for 1 minute, add the cooked ingredients and continue to stir-fry until everything is thoroughly combined. Add the sauce and cook until absorbed. Season to taste with salt and pepper.

Transfer contents of wok to a platter or a shallow bowl. Scatter with the shredded chilli, the coriander, peanuts and chilli flakes, and serve lime wedges and fish sauce separately.

SERVES 2–3 (4–6 IF SHARING SEVERAL DISHES)

Curried noodles for the new year

275 g skinless chicken breast
    fillet, diced

1 tablespoon fish sauce

½ teaspoon sugar

225 g small green (raw) prawns,
    shelled and deveined

1 teaspoon grated fresh ginger

550 g dried rice vermicelli

1 fresh red chilli, deseeded
    and sliced

1 fresh green chilli, deseeded
    and sliced

100 g fresh bean sprouts,
    blanched and drained

extra fish sauce

roasted chilli powder (see note
    page 54)

SAUCE

3 cups coconut milk

2 teaspoons minced garlic

½ cup chopped spring onions
    (reserve some of the green
    parts for garnish)

1 stem lemongrass (the pale
    green shoot end), cut in half
    lengthways

5 thick slices galangal

4 thin slices fresh ginger, cut
    into fine shreds

50 g dried salt fish, soaked for
    20 minutes in warm water

1 tablespoon shrimp paste

extra cup thick coconut milk

salt and white pepper

Combine chicken with the fish sauce and sugar, and set aside for
15 minutes. In another small dish, marinate the prawns with the grated
ginger for 10 minutes. Soak the vermicelli in warm water for 20 minutes,
then drain in a colander. ➤

To prepare the sauce, pour the 3 cups coconut milk into a saucepan and add the garlic, spring onions, lemongrass, galangal, ginger and drained salt fish. Bring to the boil, stirring slowly, then reduce heat and simmer for about 20 minutes, until a film of oil floats on the surface.

Meanwhile, roast the shrimp paste (see page 248) and scrape into the sauce. Cook a further 5 minutes, then add the thick coconut milk, plus salt and pepper to taste. Add the chicken and prawns, and simmer for 5 minutes. Finally add the noodles, chillies and bean sprouts, and heat through. Serve in bowls, with the fish sauce and roasted ground chilli on the side.

Dried, salted fish is available in Asian food stores, either hanging or packaged (often in the refrigerated section). Any unused portion will keep for ages in the fridge.

SERVES 6 (UP TO 10 IF SHARING SEVERAL DISHES)

Chicken on soba noodles

400 g dried soba noodles

225 g skinless chicken breast fillet, cubed

1 tablespoon finely minced fresh ginger

½ cup minced spring onions

1 sheet dried nori (compressed seaweed)

1 tablespoon white sesame seeds

2½ cups ichiban dashi (page 18)

¼ cup light soy sauce

1 tablespoon mirin (Japanese sweet rice wine)

2 tablespoons peanut oil

1–3 teaspoons shichimi (Japanese pepper condiment) or chilli flakes, to taste

Bring 1 litre of lightly salted water to the boil, add the noodles and return water to boil. Add ½ cup of cold water, bring back to boil and then add another ½ cup cold water. When the water again returns to boil, cook the noodles for 3 minutes, or until barely tender. Drain in a strainer, rinse under hot water, and set aside.

Place ginger on a small piece of cloth, gather the cloth around it and squeeze to extract the juice. Sprinkle juice over the chicken, set aside for 5 minutes.

Rinse the cloth, discarding the ginger. Now repeat the process with the spring onions, rinsing under cold water and then squeezing dry. >

Cut seaweed into fine shreds. Toast the sesame seeds in a dry pan over medium heat until they begin to pop.

Bring 2 litres of unsalted water to the boil, add noodles to reheat, then remove and drain well. In another saucepan bring the dashi stock, soy sauce and mirin just to the boil. Heat the oil in a frying-pan and sauté the chicken until it changes colour. Remove from the pan.

Divide noodles and chicken between four bowls. Add the rinsed spring onions, pour the hot broth over, and garnish with the shredded seaweed, sesame seeds, and a pinch of shichimi or chilli flakes.

SERVES 4

Teriyaki soba

⅓ cup sake (Japanese rice wine)

1 tablespoon mirin (Japanese sweet rice wine)

½ cup light soy sauce

2 tablespoons sugar

325 g dried soba noodles

1½ teaspoons sesame oil

275 g turkey or chicken breast fillet

12 small spring onions, trimmed and cut into 5-cm lengths

2 tablespoons vegetable oil

shichimi (Japanese pepper condiment), to serve

To make teriyaki sauce, combine the sake, mirin, soy sauce and sugar in a small bowl.

Bring 1 litre of water to the boil, add the noodles and return the water to boil. Add 1 cup of cold water, then again return water to boil, reduce heat slightly and simmer until noodles are barely tender (test them frequently after 2½ minutes). Drain in a colander, sprinkle with sesame oil, and set aside.

Slice the turkey or chicken thinly and then cut into shreds. Heat the vegetable oil in a frying-pan over high heat. Fry the chicken until cooked through (1½ minutes), then remove. >

Fry the spring onions for 1 minute, add the prepared teriyaki sauce and cook until the onions are glazed and tender. Add the chicken, and stir to glaze also.

Place noodles in a strainer and pour boiling water over to reheat. Divide noodles between four small bowls (or small lacquered boxes). Arrange the chicken and spring onions on top and sprinkle sparingly with shichimi before serving.

SERVES 4

Soy & sesame duck on noodles

½ duck (about 650 g)

2 tablespoons sesame oil

¼ cup dark soy sauce

¾ cup rice wine or dry sherry

1 × 4-cm piece fresh ginger,
   peeled and thickly sliced

1 teaspoon salt

250 g dried thin wheat noodles
   (e.g. somen)

250 g baby bok choy, halved
   lengthways

Using a cleaver to cut through the bones, chop the duck into 5-cm pieces. Heat the sesame oil in a heavy saucepan over high heat and fry the duck until skin is evenly browned. Add the soy sauce, rice wine, water and ginger to the pan, cover, and bring to the boil. Reduce the heat and simmer until duck is tender (about 35 minutes).

Bring 2 litres of water to the boil with the salt, add the noodles and cook for 3 minutes, until tender, and drain. Bring another small pan of water to the boil. Add the bok choy and boil for 3 minutes until crisp-tender, then drain.

Divide the noodles between six bowls. Place the duck and vegetables on the noodles and pour some of the broth over.

SERVES 4 (6–8 IF SHARING SEVERAL DISHES)

Quail wearing pearls
in noodle baskets

4 noodle baskets (page 232)

mixed small lettuce leaves

small sprigs or leaves of fresh
    herbs (coriander, mint, basil)

4 quail

8 shallots

1 yellow zucchini

1 green zucchini

½ choko (optional)

1 carrot

½ cup green peas

3 tablespoons vegetable oil

1 teaspoon minced fresh ginger

⅓ teaspoon minced garlic

½ cup roasted cashew nuts
    (optional)

¾ cup chicken stock

3 teaspoons cornflour

1 tablespoon hoisin sauce

1½ teaspoons chilli-bean paste

2 teaspoons rice wine or dry
    sherry

salt and freshly ground
    black pepper

QUAIL MARINADE

2 teaspoons light soy sauce

2 teaspoons hoisin sauce

1 teaspoon rice wine or dry
    sherry

1 teaspoon cornflour

Place one noodle basket on each dinner plate. Surround with the mixed
lettuce leaves and herbs. Set aside.

Cut the quail into quarters. Combine the marinade ingredients in a flat dish, add the quail and turn to coat. Set aside for 30 minutes.

Peel the shallots and cut a cross in the base of each one to prevent them from bursting during cooking. Peel the vegetables and use a melon-ball scoop to shape the zucchini and choko (if using) into balls approximately the size of the onions. Chop the carrot into similar-sized pieces. In a large pot bring 1 litre of water to the boil and cook choko, onions, carrot and peas for about 2 minutes, until almost tender. Add the zucchini and boil for 1 minute, then drain.

Heat the oil in a wok or large frying-pan over high heat and stir-fry the vegetables for 45 seconds, until glazed with the oil. Remove. Add the ginger and garlic with the marinated quail and stir-fry for about 3½ minutes, until cooked through. Meanwhile, combine the chicken stock and cornflour in a bowl.

Add the hoisin sauce, chilli-bean paste and rice wine to the wok and stir over medium–high heat for 30 seconds. Return the stir-fried vegetables to the wok, stir the cornflour mixture and add this also. Cook, stirring, over high heat until the sauce thickens and glazes the quail and vegetables. Add the cashews, along with salt and pepper to taste. Serve in the noodle baskets and take to the table at once.

SERVES 4

Noodles with beef, lamb & pork

Glazed, paper-thin slices of pork on egg noodles, Malaysian braised beef with thick wheat noodles, 'heavenly' lamb shreds on crisp-as-air fried vermicelli . . . There are myriad variations on the meat-and-noodles theme, some mildly flavoured, some challenging the palate with searing sauces, others impressing with full, rich tastes and silken textures.

Meats for noodles are quick-fried in blazing woks, or braised to melt-in-the-mouth tenderness. Sometimes all you need to do is slice up some bought cha siu (Chinese roast pork).

‹ Malay mee (page 144)

Malay mee

1 kg lean stewing beef (e.g. round or skirt)

1 onion, quartered

1 cinnamon stick

¾ teaspoon black pepper

1½ tablespoons ground coriander

1½ teaspoons ground cumin

2 teaspoons chilli flakes

1 tablespoon ground almonds or macadamia nuts

3 teaspoons minced fresh ginger

2 teaspoons minced garlic

3 tablespoons peanut or vegetable oil

¼ cup grated onion

1 tablespoon soybean paste

salt (or soy sauce) and sugar to taste

625 g fresh hokkien noodles

3 cups fresh bean sprouts

ACCOMPANIMENTS

1½ cups vegetable oil

1½ cups finely sliced shallots

2 tablespoons finely sliced garlic

1 cup finely sliced firm tofu

1 wok omelette, shredded (page 240)

¼ cup sliced spring onions

½ cup finely sliced celery

1–3 fresh red and green chillies, deseeded and finely sliced

Place beef in a saucepan with onion, cinnamon stick and pepper. Add 2 litres water and bring to the boil. Skim, then cover, reduce the heat, and simmer gently for about 1 hour. The meat should be very tender and the broth reduced to 5–6 cups. Remove meat and tear into shreds, place in a dish with a little broth to moisten, and set aside. Also set aside the broth.

Grind the coriander, cumin, chilli, nuts, ginger and garlic to a paste. Heat the oil in a saucepan over medium–high heat and fry paste and grated onion for 4 minutes, stirring constantly. Moisten with a little of the broth if mixture begins to stick to the pan. Add the meat and cook for 3–4 minutes, until coated with the spices. Add the soybean paste and cook for 1 minute more. Pour in the broth, bring to the boil, then reduce heat and simmer for 10 minutes. Check for seasonings, adding salt or soy sauce and a little sugar to taste.

Meanwhile, bring two pans of water (2 litres in one and 3 cups in the other) to the boil. Add the noodles to the larger pan and cook for 1½ minutes, then drain. Add bean sprouts to the other pan of boiling water and drain immediately.

To prepare the accompaniments, heat the oil in a wok, add the shallots and cook for about 4 minutes, until well browned. Remove with a slotted spoon. Add the garlic and fry until deeply browned, taking care it does not burn, and remove. Last, add the tofu and cook until golden. Arrange all the accompaniments on a platter or in small bowls.

Drain the noodles and divide among six deep bowls. Add the broth and meat, then the bean sprouts. Serve with the accompaniments.

SERVES 6

Spicy minced beef on rice noodles

250 g dried thin rice-stick
  noodles

3 tablespoons vegetable oil

275 g beef mince

2 teaspoons minced garlic

1 teaspoon freshly ground
  black pepper

2 tablespoons fish sauce

2½ teaspoons dark soy sauce

1 onion, finely sliced

1 tablespoon chopped fresh basil

fresh chilli sauce (page 231)

SAUCE

2 cups beef or chicken stock

2 teaspoons Thai red curry paste

2 teaspoons kecap manis
  (sweet soy sauce)

1 tablespoon cornflour

Soak the noodles in warm water for 25 minutes, then drain well and
sprinkle with a few drops of the oil to prevent them sticking.

Combine the beef mince with the garlic, pepper, fish sauce and 1 teaspoon
of the soy sauce, and set aside for 15 minutes. Mix the sauce ingredients
in a bowl and set aside.

Heat half the remaining oil in a wok over medium–high heat and stir-fry the
onion until softened and lightly golden. Add the beef and stir-fry over high
heat until lightly cooked. Add the sauce and cook over low–medium heat,
stirring frequently, until very aromatic (about 6 minutes). >

In another pan heat the rest of the oil and stir-fry the drained noodles with the remaining soy sauce until each strand is glazed and brown. Transfer to a plate. Pour the meat sauce over, and garnish with basil. Serve fresh chilli sauce on the side.

🥢 Decorate a spicy noodle dish with chilli 'flowers'. Using the point of a small paring knife, make six parallel lengthwise slits in a long, fresh red chilli, cutting right through at the tip but leaving 1 cm uncut at the base. Separate these petals, then carefully pare or scrape away the pith. Chill in iced water until the petals curl. Store in the refrigerator in a plastic container until needed.

SERVES 4 (6–8 IF SHARING SEVERAL DISHES)

Niku udon

450 g dried udon noodles
(or 675 g fresh)

100 g beef or pork fillet

2 teaspoons vegetable oil

6 dried shiitake mushrooms,
soaked for 25 minutes in
cold water

½ cup light soy sauce

½ cup ichiban dashi (page 18)

large pinch of sugar

1 onion, halved and finely sliced

8 cups Japanese noodle broth
(page 19)

3 tablespoons sliced spring
onions

1½ teaspoons shichimi
(Japanese pepper condiment)
or toasted white sesame seeds,
lightly crushed

Bring 2 litres of water to the oil. Add the noodles and cook for 1 minute, add 1 cup of water, cook until the noodles are tender, and drain. (Fresh udon take only about 3 minutes to cook; dried take about 6 minutes.)

Rub the beef with the oil. Heat a hot plate or griller to high and cook beef, turning constantly, until rare inside with a well-seared surface (about 3 minutes). Set aside.

Simmer drained mushrooms for 3–4 minutes in the soy sauce, dashi stock, and sugar. ➤

Bring 1 cup of water to the boil, add the onion, blanch for 20 seconds, then remove and rinse in cold water. Drain well. Heat the noodle broth to boiling.

Divide noodles between four deep bowls, place a serving of onion, mushrooms and spring onions in each, and pour the hot broth over. Slice beef thinly, add to bowls, scatter with sesame seeds or shichimi, and serve at once.

SERVES 4 GENEROUSLY

Sukiyaki

675 g beef sirloin or porterhouse, trimmed

250 g dried sukiyaki noodles

12 dried shiitake mushrooms, soaked for 25 minutes in warm water

6 leeks, white and pale-green parts only

6 large spring onions

400 g Chinese cabbage

325 g soft tofu

6 large eggs

2 tablespoons fresh suet (use vegetable oil, if unavailable)

SAUCE

1¼ cups niban dashi (see note page 18)

1 cup light soy sauce

¼ cup dark soy sauce

¾ cup mirin (Japanese sweet rice wine)

3 tablespoons fine sugar

Cut beef across the grain into paper-thin slices (see note page 156) and arrange them, overlapped, on a platter.

Soften the noodles in hot water and drain well. Drain the mushrooms and trim off the stems close to the cap. Cut leeks into 4-cm lengths, then cut across these at a sharp angle to produce pieces with a flat base and one sharply sloping side. Stand these on the platter and arrange the mushrooms nearby.

Cut spring onions into 4-cm lengths, discarding at least half of the green tops. Cut the cabbage into 2-cm slices, and the tofu into 2-cm cubes. **>**

Arrange spring onions, cabbage and tofu on the platter with the beef, noodles and other ingredients.

Combine sauce ingredients in a small saucepan, bring to boil, then reduce heat slightly and simmer for 1 minute. Strain into a jug and take to the table. Break an egg into each of six bowls and place at each table setting.

Heat a tabletop cooking pan (e.g. electric frypan), grease surface with suet or vegetable oil, and add a portion of the sauce. When sauce begins to bubble, the cooking can begin.

Using wooden chopsticks or fondue forks, everyone cooks their own meal: first the meat, then the vegetables and tofu, and finally the noodles; the ingredients should not swim in the sauce, but be glazed. Add a little water to the pan from time to time during the meal, as the sauce will become more concentrated as it cooks.

Dip each mouthful into the beaten egg before eating; the heat of the ingredients will partially cook the eggs so it forms a creamy coating.

SERVES 6

Heavenly lamb shreds

450 g lean lamb

3 teaspoons rice wine or
dry sherry

1 teaspoon brown sugar

1 tablespoon hoisin sauce

oil for deep-frying

50 g dried rice vermicelli

2 tablespoons vegetable oil

1½ teaspoons sesame oil

1 onion, cut into wedges

1⅓ tablespoons hoisin sauce

2 teaspoons hot chilli sauce

⅓ teaspoon salt

1 tablespoon finely shredded
orange zest

1 tablespoon finely sliced
spring-onion greens

Slice the lamb very thinly, then cut into fine shreds. Place in a bowl with the
rice wine, sugar and hoisin sauce, mix well, and cover. Marinate for 2 hours.

In a fryer or large wok, heat the deep-frying oil to 190°C. Carefully slide
the vermicelli into the pan and cook just long enough for it to expand into
a white cloud. Turn quickly before it colours, and cook the other side.
Lift into a colander lined with several layers of paper towel and set aside.

Heat the vegetable and sesame oils together in a wok over high heat,
until hazy. Add the onion and stir-fry for about 2 minutes, until well cooked.
Remove, or push to the side of the pan. Add the lamb and stir-fry for
2 minutes. Add the hoisin and chilli sauces, and the salt, and cook another
20 seconds. Remove from the heat. ➤

Spread the fried vermicelli on a platter. Spoon the spicy lamb over the noodles and garnish with the orange-zest shreds and spring-onion greens. Serve at once.

⬮ Quick-cooked Asian dishes often require fine shreds or paper-thin slices of meat. To make this easier, partially freeze the meat for about 30 minutes until it is firm enough not to wriggle as you slice it. The finer the slices are, the more tender when cooked and the more they will absorb the flavour of marinades and seasonings. For shreds, stack the slices in piles of four or five and cut across into fine slivers.

SERVES 2 (4 IF SHARING SEVERAL DISHES)

Beijing noodles

175 g lean pork mince

1½ tablespoons light soy sauce

3 teaspoons hoisin sauce

2½ teaspoons sugar

225 g dried thin wheat noodles

¼ cup vegetable oil

2 teaspoons Sichuan pepper

2 cloves garlic, peeled

1½ tablespoons fatty pork mince

2 tablespoons minced
  spring onions

1½ teaspoons minced
  fresh ginger

1 cup chicken stock

1 tablespoon cornflour

salt and pepper

hoisin sauce, to serve

Place the lean pork mince in a dish with the light soy and hoisin sauces, and the sugar, and mix well. Set aside for 20 minutes.

Bring 1.5 litres of water to the boil, add the noodles, and return the water to the boil. Add ½ cup of cold water, bring the water back to the boil again, then cook the noodles until tender, testing frequently after the first 2 minutes. Drain in a colander and set aside.

Heat the oil in a wok over high heat until hazy, add the pepper and garlic, reduce heat to medium–low, and cook for 1½ minutes. Remove with a wire ladle and discard. Increase the heat to high, add the seasoned ❯

pork and fat pork minces, and stir-fry for 3 minutes, until cooked, using a spatula to break up the meat. Add the spring onions and ginger, and stir-fry briefly.

Combine chicken stock and cornflour, pour into wok and cook over high heat, stirring constantly, until thickened. Season to taste with salt and pepper.

Divide noodles between shallow bowls and spoon sauce over. Dilute hoisin sauce with a little cold water and serve on the side.

SERVES 2–3 (6 IF SHARING SEVERAL DISHES)

Stir-fried rice ribbon noodles, Singapore-style

275 g lean pork

1 tablespoon yellow bean sauce

150 g dried wide rice noodles (or 550 g fresh)

3 tablespoons vegetable oil

140 g green (raw) prawns, shelled and deveined

3 tablespoons sliced button or straw mushrooms

⅓ cup sliced bamboo shoots

100 g spinach or water spinach leaves

1 cup chicken or beef stock

1 tablespoon cornflour

1 tablespoon dark soy sauce

2½ teaspoons white sugar

2 tablespoons chopped fresh coriander leaves

2 tablespoons spring-onion greens, sliced diagonally

Slice the pork thinly across the grain, then stack and cut into 1-cm strips. Mash the yellow bean sauce with 1 tablespoon water, pour over the pork, and marinate for 30 minutes.

Bring 1.5 litres of water to a boil, add the dried noodles and cook for about 4 minutes, until tender. (If using fresh noodles, soak in cold water for about 2 minutes, then drain.)

Heat half the oil in a wok or large frying-pan over very high heat until hazy. Stir-fry the pork for about 1½ minutes, then remove. Add the prawns, mushrooms, and bamboo shoots, and stir-fry for 1 minute. Add the spinach, stir-fry until wilted, and remove from the pan. >

Rinse out the pan and reheat with the remaining oil over highest heat. Add the drained noodles and stir-fry for about 2 minutes. Combine the stock and cornflour. Sizzle the soy sauce down the sides of the pan, add the sugar, and pour in the stock. Cook, stirring, until the sauce glazes the noodles.

Return the cooked ingredients to the wok and heat through. Stir in half the coriander and spring onions, transfer contents of wok to a dish, and garnish with the remaining coriander and onion greens. Serve at once.

When adding soy sauce or rice wine to dishes like this one, sizzle it onto the sloped inner surface of the hot wok, rather than mixing it in with the sauce ingredients. The heat of the pan brings out its fullest flavours, and adds much to the aroma of the dish.

SERVES 2–3

Pork lo mein

225 g coarse pork mince

450 g fresh thick egg noodles

¼ cup vegetable or peanut oil

1 small onion, cut into
  narrow wedges

½ red capsicum, deseeded
  and cut into strips

1 stalk celery, sliced thinly
  on the diagonal

2 spring onions, cut into
  2.5-cm lengths

8 fresh oyster mushrooms,
  halved

⅔ cup sliced bamboo shoots

1 tablespoon sesame oil

1 teaspoon Chinese black vinegar

2 tablespoons oyster sauce

1 teaspoon salt

SEASONING FOR PORK

2 teaspoons grated fresh ginger

2 cloves garlic, minced

3 teaspoons light soy sauce

3 teaspoons cornflour

1 teaspoon sugar

pinch of white pepper

1 tablespoon vegetable or
  peanut oil

SAUCE

1¼ cups chicken stock

1 tablespoon cornflour

1½ tablespoons oyster sauce

Combine pork mince with the pork seasoning in a bowl, mix well, and set
aside for 30 minutes.

Bring 2 litres of water to a boil, add the noodles and cook for about
2½ minutes, until al dente. Transfer to a colander to drain. ❯

Combine the sauce ingredients in a bowl and set aside.

Heat 2 tablespoons of the vegetable oil in a wok over high heat and stir-fry the prepared vegetables for 2–3 minutes until crisp-tender. Remove and keep warm. Add the pork and stir-fry over high heat until evenly browned, breaking it up with a spatula. Return the vegetables to the wok. Stir the sauce, pour into the wok and stir over medium heat until it begins to thicken. Transfer to a dish and set aside, keeping warm. Rinse and dry the wok.

Immerse the drained noodles in boiling water to reheat, then transfer to a colander and drain well. Heat remaining vegetable oil in the wok and stir-fry the noodles over high heat for 1 minute. Add the sesame oil, vinegar, oyster sauce and salt, and stir-fry until each strand is coated with the seasonings. Return the sauce to the wok and reheat with the noodles, mixing in evenly. Serve in bowls.

SERVES 2–3 (6 IF SHARING SEVERAL DISHES)

Tonkatsu ramen

400 g pork fillet

salt and black pepper

½ cup plain flour

2 eggs, lightly beaten

1½ cups fine, dry breadcrumbs

400 g ramen noodles

1 litre Japanese noodle broth (page 19)

oil for deep-frying

1 tablespoon sesame oil

1 tablespoon finely sliced spring-onion greens

tonkatsu sauce (page 238)

Slice pork into 8 rounds, then pound the slices until about 5 mm thick. Season with salt and pepper, and coat lightly with flour. Dip into beaten eggs and coat with breadcrumbs.

Bring a pan of water to the boil, add noodles and simmer for about 4 minutes, until tender. Drain and set aside. Heat the noodle broth in another pan. Meanwhile, heat the oils to 190°C in a pan suitable for deep-frying. Lower pork pieces into the oil and cook until coating is crunchy and golden-brown (about 5 minutes). Remove, drain on absorbent paper, then cut into slices 10 mm wide.

Divide the noodles among four bowls. Add broth (do not cover the noodles, as this will make the crumbed pork soggy). Sprinkle with spring-onion greens, top with pork pieces and drizzle with tonkatsu sauce before serving.

SERVES 4

Pork & snake beans
on soft-fried egg noodles

225 g pork fillet

2 tablespoons light soy sauce

1 teaspoon white sugar

225 g snake beans or
    green beans

1 onion, cut into narrow wedges

350 g dried thin egg noodles

3 tablespoons vegetable oil

6 slices fresh ginger,
    finely shredded

1 teaspoon minced garlic

1 cup chicken stock

2½ teaspoons cornflour

1½ tablespoons oyster sauce

Slice the pork thinly across the grain and place in a dish. Add 1 tablespoon of the soy sauce, and the sugar, mix well and set aside.

Cut the beans into 4-cm lengths, and separate onion wedges into layers.

Bring 2 litres of water to the boil and salt sparingly. Add the noodles and bring back to the boil. Reduce heat slightly and cook for 3½ minutes, until al dente. Drain in a colander.

Heat 1 tablespoon of the oil in a wok over medium heat and stir-fry the beans for 30 seconds. Add 1 tablespoon of cold water, cover the pan and cook for 1½–2 minutes. Remove to a plate. Rinse and dry the pan, then reheat over high heat with another tablespoon of the oil and stir-fry the onion until barely tender. Remove. ❯

Heat the remaining oil over very high heat, add the noodles and stir-fry until each strand is glazed. Transfer to a serving plate. Stir-fry the pork in the same pan, adding the ginger and garlic. When the pork changes colour (about 1 minute), sizzle the remaining tablespoon of soy sauce onto the sides of the pan.

Return the beans and onions to the wok, and stir-fry for 30 seconds. Combine the stock and cornflour and pour into the pan. Cook, stirring, over high heat until the sauce glazes the meat. Arrange over the noodles, drizzle with the oyster sauce, and serve at once.

SERVES 3–4 (6–8 IF SHARING SEVERAL DISHES)

Sweet pork & onions on noodles

175 g pork fillet

4 tablespoons vegetable oil

150 g dried thin egg noodles

1 onion, cut into narrow wedges

2 teaspoons rice wine or
　dry sherry

1 tablespoon hoisin sauce

2 teaspoons light soy sauce

¼ red capsicum or I large, fresh
　red chilli, deseeded and
　finely shredded

½ cup chicken stock

salt and white pepper

1⅓ teaspoons cornflour

SEASONING FOR PORK

2½ teaspoons light soy sauce

1 teaspoon rice wine or
　dry sherry

1 teaspoon cornflour

Cut the pork into paper-thin slices, then into strips 5 cm × 2.5 cm. Place in a bowl, add the pork seasoning ingredients, mix well, and set aside for 20 minutes to marinate.

Bring 1.5 litres of lightly salted water to the boil with 1½ teaspoons of the oil. Add the noodles and reheat to boiling, stirring to untangle the bundles. Reduce heat to a simmer and cook for another 3 minutes, until al dente. Drain and set aside.

Heat half the remaining oil in a wok over high heat. Stir-fry the noodles for 30 seconds, keeping them constantly moving. Transfer to a plate. ❯

Heat the rest of the oil until a haze forms, add the onion and stir-fry until softened (about 1 minute), then push to the side of the pan. Add the pork slices and stir-fry over high heat until they change colour (about 1 minute).

Sizzle the rice wine onto the sides of the wok, add the hoisin and light soy sauces. Add the capsicum and stir-fry until the meat is glazed with the sauce. Combine the stock, salt, pepper and cornflour, add to the wok and stir until the sauce thickens and clears. Pour over the noodles and serve at once.

SERVES 2

Vegetables & chilled noodle dishes

You don't need to be a vegetarian to enjoy these delicious vegetable dishes!

Braised in a clay pot with mushrooms, tofu and vegetables, wok-tossed with green beans and peanuts, stir-fried with tender Chinese cabbage, or bathed in a fiery chilli sauce, vegetable noodle dishes are substantial, nourishing and colourful. And for meat-eaters, the recipes here would also accept the addition of shredded meat, poultry or seafood.

Soba, the Japanese buckwheat noodles with a unique nutty flavour, are a particular favourite for chilled noodle dishes. So too are bean threads and sukiyaki noodles, which both retain their appealing crunch. The refreshing salads in this section can be served on their own in hot weather, as a first course, or with a variety of dishes in the Asian style.

‹ 'Gazing at the moon' soba (page 174)

'Gazing at the moon' soba

4 large shiitake mushrooms
(if dried, soak for 15 minutes
in cold water)

400 g dried soba noodles

175 g baby spinach leaves

2 spring onions, sliced
diagonally into 4-cm lengths

4 eggs

BROTH

4 cups ichiban dashi (page 18)

1½ tablespoons mirin
(Japanese sweet rice wine)

1 tablespoon sake
(Japanese rice wine)

¼ cup light soy sauce

sugar and salt to taste

Remove dried mushrooms (if using) from the cold water, drain and then place in a small bowl and pour ½ cup boiling water over (this is to remove any grit, as soaking liquid will be reused). Set aside for 15 minutes, then drain again, reserving the liquid. Remove the stems and slice caps into fine shreds.

Bring 5 cups of water to the boil. Add the noodles and return the water to the boil. Add 1 cup of cold water and bring back to the boil, then add ½ cup of cold water and bring back to the boil again. Repeat the process one more time, then reduce the heat slightly and simmer until noodles are al dente. Drain at once, rinse under cold water, then drain again and set aside.

Rinse the spinach, drain, and place in a small saucepan with only the water still clinging to the leaves. Cover and cook over low heat for a minute or so, until wilted, shaking the pan occasionally. Wrap several leaves together around a pair of chopsticks to make four small bundles.

Reheat the noodles in boiling water, drain, and divide among four bowls. Heat the broth ingredients to boiling, adding the reserved mushroom-soaking liquid, then pour over the noodles. In each bowl, arrange mushroom slices, a bundle of spinach, and several pieces of spring onion (place them to the side, to allow room for the egg). Make a shallow depression in the noodles, break 1 egg into each bowl and serve immediately (the egg will partially cook in the hot broth).

You can poach the spinach in the broth. Place the leaves in a small saucepan and add broth to barely cover, cook gently for about 4 minutes, strain the broth back into the pot, and bundle the spinach as described in the recipe.

SERVES 4

Indonesian-style vermicelli in coconut sauce

2 tablespoons peanut oil

1 cup finely chopped onion

4 cloves garlic, minced

1 fresh red chilli, deseeded and minced

2 stalks lemongrass, trimmed and halved lengthways

2 teaspoons minced fresh ginger

1 tablespoon ground coriander

1 teaspoon ground cumin

1 teaspoon ground laos

½ teaspoon freshly ground black pepper

¾ teaspoon shrimp paste (optional)

1 teaspoon soft brown sugar

3 curry leaves (optional)

3 cups coconut milk

3 cups vegetable stock

2 large potatoes, peeled and sliced

225 g green beans, cut into 5-cm lengths

2 small carrots, peeled and sliced

175 g dried rice vermicelli

extra 1½ tablespoons peanut oil

120 g firm tofu, sliced

450 g Chinese cabbage, sliced

1½ cups fresh bean sprouts

4 spring onions, cut into 4-cm lengths

2 tablespoons chopped fresh coriander leaves

1 tablespoon chopped fresh basil

freshly squeezed lime juice

salt and black pepper

fish sauce and soy sauce, to taste

To make the coconut sauce, heat the peanut oil in a wok over medium heat and stir-fry the onion until softened and golden-brown (about 4 minutes). >

Add the garlic, chilli, lemongrass and ginger to the wok, sauté briefly, then add the spices and stir. Mash the shrimp paste against the side of the pan and stir in, then add the sugar, curry leaves and coconut milk. Bring to boil and simmer for about 12 minutes, until a film of oil floats on the surface. Add the stock, potatoes, beans and carrots, and cook until vegetables are barely tender (about 10 minutes).

Meanwhile, soak the vermicelli in warm water for 8 minutes, then drain thoroughly. Heat the extra peanut oil in a small pan and fry the tofu until golden. Use a slotted spoon to transfer it to the sauce along with the noodles, cabbage, bean sprouts, spring onions and half the chopped coriander. Cook for 3–4 minutes, then add the basil leaves. Check the seasonings, adding salt, black pepper, lime juice and fish sauce or soy sauce to taste. Serve in deep dishes, garnished with the reserved coriander.

You can substitute vegetable oil for the peanut oil, and yellow bean sauce (2–3 teaspoons) can be used instead of shrimp paste.

SERVES 4–6

Seaweed & fried tofu on udon

675 g fresh udon noodles

15 g dried wakame (curly seaweed), soaked for 25 minutes in warm water

2 litres Japanese noodle broth (page 19)

4 pieces fried tofu (see note page 126)

3 tablespoons fresh nameko mushrooms

½ cup sliced spring-onion greens

2 tablespoons shredded nori (compressed seaweed)

shichimi (Japanese pepper condiment), to taste

Bring 2 litres of water to the boil, add the noodles, cook for about 2½ minutes, until tender, and drain. Drain the seaweed and cut into small pieces about 2.5 cm × 1 cm. Heat noodle broth, add the seaweed and simmer for 5 minutes.

Place tofu in a dish, pour boiling water over, soak for a few minutes, then drain and squeeze out excess water. Dry between pieces of paper towel. Cut the bean curd into thin slices.

Divide the noodles among four deep bowls. Pour the broth and seaweed over, and add the bean curd, mushrooms and spring onions. Before serving, scatter with nori shreds and add shichimi to taste.

SERVES 4

Singaporean vegetable chow mein

200 g dried thin egg noodles

3 dried shiitake mushrooms,
  soaked for 20 minutes in
  warm water

8 small broccoli florets

3 tablespoons vegetable oil

1 small carrot, peeled and thinly
  sliced diagonally

1 stalk celery, thinly sliced
  diagonally

8 snow or sugar-snap peas,
  stemmed

¼ cup sliced bamboo shoots,
  rinsed and drained

1½ cups fresh bean sprouts

120 g firm tofu, thinly sliced

1 teaspoon minced ginger

½ teaspoon minced garlic

2 tablespoons minced
  spring onions

fresh coriander leaves
  for garnish

SAUCE

1½ tablespoons light soy sauce

⅓ teaspoon chilli oil

½ teaspoon sugar

salt and freshly ground pepper

¾ cup water or vegetable stock

3 teaspoons cornflour

Bring 2.5 litres of salted water to the boil. Add the noodles, bring back to boil, and stir to untangle the bundles. Reduce heat and cook with the water barely bubbling for about 3 minutes, until al dente. Drain, rinse with cold water, and drain again. Set aside. >

Drain the mushrooms, squeeze out excess water, trim off the stems and cut caps into narrow strips. Blanch the broccoli in boiling water for 1 minute, drain, refresh under running cold water, and drain again.

Mix the sauce ingredients in a bowl and set aside.

Heat the oil in a wok or large frying-pan. Add all the vegetables except the bean sprouts, stir-fry for 2 minutes, and remove. Next, stir-fry the noodles over maximum heat for 1½ minutes, until well coated with the oil (add a little extra oil if needed). Remove to a serving plate.

Add the ginger, garlic and spring onions to the pan and cook until aromatic (about 45 seconds). Stir the sauce, pour into the pan, and cook until it begins to thicken. Return the vegetables to the pan and add the bean sprouts and tofu. Heat thoroughly, stirring until the ingredients are well mixed. Serve over the noodles and garnish with the fresh coriander.

SERVES 3–4

Great gravy noodles

5 dried shiitake mushrooms

1 × 5-cm piece dried black
fungus (wood ears)

175 g dried thin noodles

120 g firm tofu

40 g dried bean-curd skin,
soaked for 25 minutes in
warm water

2 tablespoons dried shrimp
(optional), soaked for
25 minutes

½ cup finely sliced fresh
straw mushrooms

6 cups vegetable stock

2½ tablespoons light soy sauce
(or fish sauce)

1 tablespoon rice wine or
dry sherry

1 teaspoon salt

1 stalk celery, julienned

⅔ cup sliced bamboo shoots,
julienned

3½ tablespoons cornflour

2–3 eggs (optional)

salt and freshly ground
black pepper to taste

sesame oil

Soak the shiitake mushrooms and black fungus in warm water for
25 minutes. Meanwhile, bring 1 litre of water to a boil and cook the
noodles for about 3½ minutes, until tender. Drain and set aside.

Drain the shiitake mushrooms, trim off stems and cut caps into fine shreds.
Drain the fungus and cut into fine shreds also. Slice the tofu thinly, then ❯

stack and cut into narrow strips. Drain the bean-curd skin and cut into noodle-like strips. Drain the shrimp.

To prepare the gravy, bring stock to the boil and add the soy sauce, rice wine and salt. Add the dried and fresh mushrooms, fungus, tofu, bean-curd skin and dried shrimp (if using), and simmer over medium heat for 12 minutes. Add the celery and bamboo shoots, and simmer for another 3 minutes. Moisten the cornflour with a little cold water, stir into the gravy, and cook until mixture thickens slightly.

If you are adding eggs, beat and strain them, then pour into the gravy in a thin stream and cook until set in threads. Check seasonings, adding salt, pepper and extra soy or fish sauce to taste. Add the noodles and heat thoroughly, then pour into deep bowls and sprinkle with a few drops of sesame oil. Serve hot.

SERVES 4

Cantonese-style vegetable noodles

4 dried shiitake mushrooms, soaked for 20 minutes

275 g dried thin wheat noodles (e.g. somen)

3½ tablespoons vegetable oil

200 g firm tofu, cubed

1 onion, finely sliced

1 small carrot, finely sliced diagonally

½ stalk celery, finely sliced diagonally

1 cup cauliflower or broccoli florets, blanched

3 Chinese cabbage leaves, sliced

1½ tablespoons light soy sauce

1½ teaspoons rice wine or dry sherry

2 cups vegetable stock

2 tablespoons cornflour

salt and white pepper

1 tablespoon chopped fresh coriander leaves

Drain the mushrooms, squeeze out excess water, trim off the stems and cut caps into thin slices.

Bring 1.5 litres of lightly salted water to the boil, add the noodles and cook for about 4 minutes, until al dente. Drain.

Heat the oil in a wok or heavy frying-pan over high heat and stir-fry the tofu for about 1½ minutes. Remove with a slotted spoon and set aside. Pour half the oil into a small dish, for later use. Reheat the wok and fry the noodles for 2 minutes over high heat, stirring and tossing to coat with oil. Remove to a serving plate. ❯

Return reserved oil to wok if needed. Over high heat stir-fry the mushrooms, onion, carrot, celery, and cauliflower or broccoli until cooked but still crunchy. Add the cabbage and cook until it wilts, then return tofu to the pan. Sizzle the soy sauce and rice wine into the pan and stir. Combine the stock and cornflour and pour into the pan. Cook, stirring, over high heat until thickened. Season to taste with salt and pepper. Pour over the noodles and garnish with the chopped coriander.

SERVES 6

Bean-thread noodles with cabbage

150 g bean-thread vermicelli

2 tablespoons vegetable oil

1 tablespoon sesame oil

160 g firm tofu, thinly sliced

2 teaspoons minced garlic

1 stalk celery, finely sliced
   diagonally

1 carrot, finely sliced diagonally

2 eggs, lightly beaten (optional)

4 spring onions, cut into
   2.5-cm lengths

3 cups finely sliced
   Chinese cabbage

2–3 tablespoons fish sauce or
   soy sauce

salt and ground black pepper

Soak the vermicelli in warm water for 15 minutes, then drain and set aside.

Heat the oils in a wok over high heat. Stir-fry the tofu with the garlic for 2 minutes until tofu is crisp at the edges, then push to the side of the pan. Add the celery and carrot, and stir-fry for 2–3 minutes, until crisp-tender. Remove ingredients from wok and set aside. If including the eggs, add them to the wok and cook until they begin to firm up underneath, then turn over and break into small pieces with a spatula.

Add noodles, spring onions and cabbage to the wok along with the previously cooked ingredients. Stir-fry over high heat until cabbage is tender and everything is well blended. Add the fish sauce, plus salt and pepper to taste.

SERVES 4 (6 IF SHARING SEVERAL DISHES)

Vegetable pad thai

SAUCE

1½ cups water

1 tablespoon tamarind
concentrate

⅓ cup dark-brown sugar

1½ tablespoons fish sauce or
light soy sauce

NOODLES

275 g dried rice-stick noodles,
(or 675 g fresh rice ribbon
noodles)

4 tablespoons peanut or
vegetable oil

300 g firm tofu, cubed

3 shallots, finely sliced

¾ teaspoon minced garlic

1 tablespoon finely chopped
dried shrimp (optional)

⅓ cup unsalted roasted peanuts

3 spring onions, cut into
2.5-cm lengths

2 cups fresh bean sprouts,
blanched and drained

1 wok omelette (optional;
page 240)

1 fresh red chilli, deseeded
and sliced

lime wedges

fine sugar

garlic chives, cut into
4-cm lengths

roasted chilli powder
(see note page 54)

fish sauce or light soy sauce

Combine sauce ingredients in a small saucepan, bring to boil and simmer
until reduced to approximately ¾ cup. Set aside to cool. >

If using dried noodles, boil for about 2 minutes until firm-tender, then drain. If using fresh, rinse in warm water and drain.

Heat the oil in a wok over high heat until hazy, add tofu cubes and fry for about 2½ minutes, until the surface is golden-brown, and remove. Pour off half the oil and reserve, and discard the other half. Add the shallots and stir-fry for 1½ minutes over high heat. Add the garlic, dried shrimp, peanuts and spring onions, and stir-fry for 1½ minutes. Stir in the bean sprouts and cook briefly, then transfer to a plate and set aside.

Wipe out the wok and add the reserved oil. When it is very hot, add the noodles and stir-fry for 2 minutes until each strand is coated with oil. Add the prepared sauce and cook until partially absorbed (about 1½ minutes). Return stir-fried ingredients to the wok, stirring to mix them evenly into the noodles, and cook until thoroughly heated. Mound the noodles on a plate and garnish with the shredded omelette and other accompaniments, serving the chilli powder and fish or soy sauce separately in small dishes.

Eggless Chinese noodles can be used in this recipe. To convert it to a non-vegetarian meal, substitute diced chicken for the tofu.

SERVES 4

Rice sticks with tofu & vegetables

275 g dried rice-stick noodles

5 tablespoons peanut or
vegetable oil

1½ cups soft tofu

1½ teaspoons minced garlic

1 carrot, diced and parboiled

½ diced cucumber, blanched

SAUCE

2 tablespoons fish sauce or light
soy sauce

1½ teaspoons tomato paste

1 tablespoon soft brown sugar

¼ cup vegetable stock or water

ACCOMPANIMENTS

2 cups fresh bean sprouts

3 spring onions, chopped

2 tablespoons chopped
roasted peanuts

2 teaspoons minced fresh
red chilli

½ cup fresh coriander leaves

fish sauce or light soy sauce

freshly squeezed lime juice, or
lime wedges

fresh chilli sauce (page 231)

Bring 1.5 litres of water to the boil, add the noodles and cook for
1½ minutes, until al dente. Pour into a colander to drain, and cool under
running cold water.

Mix the sauce ingredients in a small bowl and set aside.

Heat the oil in a wok over high heat and fry the tofu until golden-brown and
crisp on the surface. Remove with a slotted spoon. ❯

Pour off most of the oil into a heatproof dish and set aside. Reheat the pan and stir-fry the garlic for 45 seconds. Add the carrot and cucumber, and stir-fry until glazed with the oil. Remove.

Reheat the reserved oil and when smoky-hot, stir-fry the noodles to heat through. Add the sauce and cook until absorbed by the noodles, then return tofu and vegetables, and mix in evenly, cooking for 45 seconds.

Mound the noodles on a serving plate and surround or top with the prepared accompaniments. Serve the fish or soy sauce, lime juice and chilli sauce in small dishes, to be added to taste.

To cut soft tofu into even-sized cubes that won't collapse, hold the block in the palm of your hand and gently cut downward with a knife that is not excessively sharp. Slide the cubes from your hand directly into the wok or pan.

SERVES 2–3 (4–6 IF SHARING SEVERAL DISHES)

Yamakake noodles

400 g dried soba or udon
noodles

½ cup chopped and rinsed
spring onions (see note
page 91)

½ cup shredded nori
(compressed seaweed)

80 g kamaboko (Japanese fish
cake), thinly sliced

¾ cup finely grated Asian yam
(omit if unavailable)

3 cups niban dashi (see note
page 18)

DIPPING SAUCE

¼ cup light soy sauce

2 tablespoons mirin
(Japanese sweet rice wine)

1 tablespoon sugar

Bring 2 litres of water to the boil, add the noodles and cook until barely
tender (test frequently after 2½ minutes). Drain well and divide among
four bowls.

Add spring onions, nori and fish cake to each bowl and place a spoonful
of the grated yam on top, if using. Combine the sauce ingredients, bring
to the boil, and simmer for 3–4 minutes. Pour into a jug to cool.

Heat the dashi stock to boiling and pour over the noodles. Pour a little of
the dipping sauce into a small dish for each guest. Serve the noodles hot,
or allow to cool to room temperature.

SERVES 4

Plump Thai noodles
in sweet brown sauce

500 g fresh thick egg noodles

1⅓ teaspoons salt

2½ cups fresh bean sprouts

¾ cup spinach or water spinach leaves

3 spring onions

3 tablespoons peanut oil or vegetable oil

2 large eggs, lightly beaten (optional)

1 × 1-cm piece fresh ginger, finely shredded

sprigs of fresh coriander

shredded fresh red chilli

SAUCE

¾ cup vegetable stock

1½ tablespoons dark soy sauce

2 tablespoons light soy sauce

1 tablespoon soft brown sugar

½ teaspoon shrimp paste, or 1½ teaspoons soybean paste

Bring 2 litres of water to the boil, add the noodles and salt and cook for 1 minute. Remove, and drain well.

Blanch the bean sprouts in boiling water for 30 seconds, drain immediately, and cool under running cold water. Cut the spinach into 5-cm pieces, blanch for 30 seconds in boiling water, drain and refresh in cold water, then drain again and set aside. Cut the white parts of the spring onions into 2.5-cm lengths (reserve the green tops for another recipe).

Combine the sauce ingredients in a bowl and set aside.

If including the eggs, use 2 teaspoons of the oil to grease the surface of a wok. Heat to medium, pour in the eggs, and cook until they begin to set. Break into small pieces with a spatula, cook until just firm, and remove.

Add remaining oil to the wok and reheat over very high heat. Stir-fry the noodles for 2 minutes, and remove. Reduce heat slightly, add the ginger, bean sprouts, spinach and spring onions, and stir-fry for 1 minute. Return the noodles to the pan, and mix well.

Stir the sauce, pour over the noodles and cook until absorbed. Stir in the chopped egg, garnish with coriander sprigs and chilli shreds, and serve.

SERVES 2 (4–6 IF SHARING SEVERAL DISHES)

Tibetan vegetable vermicelli

1 tablespoon dried black fungus
  (wood ears)

4 dried shiitake mushrooms

225 g dried bean-thread
  vermicelli

¼ cup vegetable or peanut oil

1 onion, finely sliced

2 cloves garlic, minced

2 teaspoons minced fresh ginger

1 tablespoon sesame oil

1 fresh red chilli, deseeded
  and shredded

2–3 cups shredded
  Chinese cabbage

2 spring onions, minced

SAUCE

2½ tablespoons light soy sauce

2 teaspoons dark soy sauce

1–2 teaspoons chilli oil

1 teaspoon sugar

1 teaspoon Chinese
  brown vinegar

½ cup water

Soak the black fungus and shiitake mushrooms in hot water for 25 minutes.
Drain. Finely shred the fungus; trim off the shiitake stems and shred the
caps finely. Soak the vermicelli for 15 minutes in warm water.

Combine the sauce ingredients in a bowl and set aside.

Heat the vegetable oil in a wok over medium–high heat and stir-fry the
onion until it begins to soften. Add the garlic and ginger, stir-fry briefly
and then add the fungus, mushrooms, sesame oil, chilli and cabbage.
Stir-fry for 1–2 minutes. >

Add the noodles and prepared sauce, and stir over moderately high heat for 2–3 minutes. Transfer to a plate, scatter with the spring onions, and serve.

This recipe is a good one in which to use a variety of mushrooms. Include sliced straw mushrooms, wild mushrooms, fresh shiitake and oyster mushrooms, using with or instead of the fungus.

SERVES 2–3 (MORE IF SHARING SEVERAL DISHES)

Soba soup noodles with leeks

375 g dried soba noodles
1 tablespoon white sesame seeds
3 small leeks (or 4 large spring onions)
5 cups Japanese noodle broth (page 19)
salt

Bring 1 litre of water to the boil. Add the noodles and, when the water boils again, 1 cup cold water. When it boils again, add a final cup of water. Cook the noodles until al dente (about 3 minutes), then remove and drain.

Toast sesame seeds in a dry nonstick pan over medium heat until they are aromatic, golden and beginning to pop. Remove. Cut leeks or spring onions into 7-cm lengths, cut in half lengthways and then slice into very fine shreds.

Combine broth ingredients in a saucepan and bring to a boil. Reduce the heat and keep warm.

Transfer the noodles to a strainer, immerse in boiling water to reheat, then drain well. Divide among four warmed bowls, pour the broth over, and garnish with leek shreds and sesame seeds.

SERVES 4

Sichuan dry-fried green beans on noodles

175 g dried bean-thread noodles

225 g green beans, cut into 2.5-cm lengths

2 tablespoons vegetable oil

1 teaspoon sesame oil

1 tablespoon minced garlic

125 g fried tofu, very finely minced

1 spring onion, minced

1½ tablespoons crushed roasted peanuts or macadamias (optional)

extra cubes of fried tofu, for garnish (optional)

SAUCE

½ cup vegetable stock

1 teaspoon dark soy sauce

2 teaspoons light soy sauce

1 teaspoon chilli oil

1 teaspoon chilli-bean paste or sambal ulek

1⅓ teaspoons sugar

Bring 1.5 litres of water to the boil, add noodles and cook for about 3 minutes, until tender. Drain.

Boil beans in lightly salted water for 2½ minutes, and drain well. Heat the oils together in a wok. Stir-fry the beans for 2½–3 minutes, until they begin to wrinkle. Add the garlic, tofu and spring onion, and stir-fry for about 3 minutes until tofu is crisp and beans are cooked. >

Combine the sauce ingredients in a bowl and pour into the wok. Cook over high heat, stirring, for 1½ minutes. Add the noodles, stir to mix well, and cook over medium heat until noodles are heated through. Transfer to bowls and scatter the peanuts over the top. Add extra fried tofu cubes for garnish, if you like.

SERVES 2 (4–5 IF SHARING SEVERAL DISHES)

Bean-curd 'noodles'

2 large sheets dried
  bean-curd skin

6 × 4-cm cubes fried tofu

6 dried shiitake mushrooms,
  soaked in hot water for
  20 minutes

3 tablespoons vegetable or
  peanut oil

1½ teaspoons sesame oil

⅓ cup sliced straw mushrooms

⅓ cup sliced bamboo shoots

4 cups fresh bean sprouts

2 tablespoons chopped
  spring onions

SEASONINGS

1 teaspoon finely chopped salted
  black beans

1 tablespoon light soy sauce

1 teaspoon rice wine or dry
  sherry

1 teaspoon minced fresh ginger

⅓ teaspoon chilli oil (optional)

salt and freshly ground
  black pepper

Soak the bean-curd skins in cold water to soften (about 3 minutes),
then lift out carefully onto a cloth to dry. Roll up and cut into narrow strips.
Slice the fried tofu thinly and then cut the slices into strips. Drain the
soaked mushrooms, remove the stems, and cut caps into narrow strips.

Heat the oils in a wok over very high heat. Stir-fry the fried bean curd
for 2 minutes, until golden-brown. Add the dried and fresh mushrooms,
bamboo shoots and bean sprouts, and stir-fry for 1 minute. Remove and
set aside. ➤

Add the bean curd and noodles to the pan, and stir-fry for about 1 minute. Return fried ingredients, add the seasonings and stir them into the dish over high heat for about 1 minute. Season to taste with salt and pepper, and transfer to bowls or a serving plate. Garnish with the spring onions.

SERVES 2

Noodle salad platter

100 g dried rice vermicelli

225 g cha siu (Chinese roast pork: page 230)

225 g cooked chicken

225 g shelled, cooked prawns

2 small Japanese or Lebanese cucumbers

1 red onion, thinly sliced

1 cup fresh herb leaves (mint, basil, coriander)

mixed lettuce leaves

2 tablespoons chopped roasted peanuts

1½ tablespoons pickled garlic, finely sliced

3–4 tablespoons spring-onion oil (see note page 212)

WRAPS

8–12 Vietnamese *banh trang* (rice-paper sheets)

⅓ cup nuoc cham (Vietnamese sauce: page 235), for dipping

Soak the vermicelli in hot water for 7 minutes, drain and cut into 5-cm lengths. Slice the pork and chicken thinly, then stack slices and cut into narrow strips. Cut the prawns in half lengthways.

Cut the cucumbers in half lengthways, then into thin slices. Combine the meats, prawns, cucumber, onion and half the herbs.

Arrange the lettuce and vermicelli on a platter. Pile the combined salad ingredients on top and scatter with the peanuts and pickled garlic. Garnish with the remaining herbs and pour on the spring-onion oil just before serving. >

Alternatively, guests can wrap the salad in rice-paper sheets. If so, first sprinkle fried spring onions and some of their oil evenly over the salad to moisten the ingredients. Soften the rice-paper sheets by dipping in cold water, then spread on a kitchen towel. Invite guests to place a generous portion of salad in the centre of each sheet and roll it up. Dip into the nuoc cham, and eat.

Spring-onion oil is a delicious dressing for many Vietnamese dishes. To make it, trim and chop a small bunch of spring onions. Heat ½ cup mild-flavoured oil over a medium flame and fry the spring onions for about 1½ minutes, until they have softened. Remove and cool. The oil can be refrigerated for at least 1 week.

SERVES 4–6

Cold sesame noodles on char-grilled vegetables

175 g dried thin or flat
egg noodles

225 g cooked chicken
breast fillet

1 medium-sized slender
eggplant, finely sliced

1 yellow zucchini, finely sliced

1 green zucchini, finely sliced

2 small Japanese or Lebanese
cucumbers, julienned

1/2 red capsicum, deseeded
and julienned

6 sugar or snow peas, blanched
for 30 seconds

1 spring onion, shredded

olive oil

salt and freshly ground
black pepper

SESAME SAUCE

2 tablespoons tahini

1 1/2 tablespoons light olive oil
or vegetable oil

1 3/4 teaspoons sesame oil

3 1/2 teaspoons mirin (Japanese
sweet rice wine)

1 1/2 tablespoons minced
spring onion

1/2 teaspoon minced garlic

Cook the noodles in 1.5 litres of slightly salted boiling water until al dente. Drain, cover with cold water to cool, then drain again.

Cut the chicken into narrow strips. Spread the eggplant and zucchini slices on a tray, sprinkle with salt, and set aside for 10 minutes to draw off any bitter juices. ➤

Preheat griller to hot. Combine the sauce ingredients in a bowl, adding cold water to dilute to a creamy consistency. Pour half the dressing over the drained noodles, mix to distribute evenly, and set aside.

Wipe the eggplant and zucchini dry and brush with olive oil. Grill until well cooked, with a smoky aroma (about 1½ minutes a side). Sprinkle with a little more olive oil, and season with salt and a few twists from the pepper mill. Set aside.

Mix the chicken, cucumber, pepper, peas and spring onion with the noodles and serve in a mound in the centre of each serving plate. Fan the grilled vegetable around the noodles and pour the remaining sauce over.

You can also use dried soba or somen noodles for this dish. Smooth peanut butter can be substituted for the tahini.

SERVES 2 (MORE AS AN APPETISER)

Glass-noodle salad

100 g fine bean-thread noodles

3 cloves garlic, finely sliced

6 shallots, peeled and
finely sliced

100 g firm tofu, cut into
very small dice

⅓ cup vegetable oil

1 cup finely sliced
Chinese cabbage

1 cup finely sliced cos lettuce

1 stalk celery, finely sliced
diagonally

1 small carrot, finely sliced
diagonally

1 cup coarsely grated unripe
(green) pawpaw or mango

1–2 fresh green chillies,
deseeded and minced

1 red onion, finely sliced

¼ cup loosely packed fresh
coriander leaves

DRESSING

¼ cup fish sauce or
light soy sauce

¼ cup freshly squeezed
lime juice

1½ teaspoons dark-brown sugar

2 teaspoons toasted white sesame
seeds or finely chopped
roasted peanuts

Soak noodles in warm water to soften, drain thoroughly, and then cut into
7-cm lengths.   ➤

Fry the garlic, shallots and tofu in the oil over high heat until crisp and golden-brown, then leave on absorbent paper to drain (reserve the oil to add to the dressing). Whisk the dressing ingredients together, adding oil to taste, until emulsified. Set aside.

Combine remaining vegetables in a large bowl. Add the noodles, the fried ingredients and the dressing, and toss thoroughly. Serve piled high on a platter.

SERVES 4–6

Classic cold soba

450 g dried soba or cha soba
  noodles

2 teaspoons sesame oil

½ sheet nori (compressed
  seaweed)

1 tablespoon wasabi powder
  or paste

¾ cup chopped spring onions

1 × 5-cm piece fresh ginger, very
  finely grated

DIPPING SAUCE

1½ cups water

¾ cup lightly packed
  bonito flakes

⅓ cup light soy sauce

3 tablespoons mirin (Japanese
  sweet rice wine)

2 teaspoons caster sugar

Bring 2 litres of water to the boil, add the noodles and bring water back
to boil. Pour in 1 cup of cold water and return to the boil. Add another cup
of cold water, return to the boil, and cook for about 3 minutes, until the
noodles are al dente. Drain, rinse under running cold water, and drain again.
Transfer to a bowl and sprinkle with the sesame oil, then cover and chill.

Toast the nori over a flame until it turns bright green and feels crisp, then
cut into fine shreds. If using wasabi powder, mix it to a paste with cold
water and a little sake.

Combine the sauce ingredients in a saucepan, bring to the boil, then
reduce heat and simmer for 3 minutes. Remove from the heat and leave
to cool, then strain through a fine sieve and chill.

Serve the noodles in tangles on flat cane baskets, lacquered trays or chilled plates (brush the plates with sesame oil to prevent noodles sticking). Scatter the shredded nori on top and give each diner a small tray containing a little dish of spring onions, a mound of ginger, a portion of wasabi, and a bowl of the dipping sauce.

SERVES 4

Mushroom soba salad

225 g dried soba or hiyamugi
   noodles

2 teaspoons sesame oil

12 large dried shiitake
   mushrooms, soaked for
   30 minutes

2 cups ichiban dashi (page 18)

2 teaspoons sugar

3 thin slices fresh ginger

1 tablespoon light soy sauce

12 spinach leaves, rinsed

100 g fresh enoki mushrooms,
   drained

2 tablespoons finely sliced
   preserved pink ginger

DRESSING

⅓ cup mirin (Japanese sweet
   rice wine)

⅓ cup dark soy sauce

2 tablespoons bonito flakes

Bring 1.5 litres of water to the boil, add the noodles, and cook until tender.
Drain well, then sprinkle with the sesame oil and set aside.

Drain the soaked mushrooms and trim off the stems. Place caps in a small
saucepan with the dashi stock, sugar, ginger and soy sauce. Bring to the
boil, reduce heat to medium, partially cover the pan and cook for 20 minutes.
Remove the mushrooms with a slotted spoon, cut into fine strips and set
aside. Strain cooking liquid through a fine strainer and discard the ginger.

Reheat mushroom stock, add the spinach leaves, poach for 1 minute, and
remove with a strainer. Strain the stock again if necessary. There should
be 1 cup of liquid. >

To make the dressing, boil the mirin in a small saucepan until reduced by half. Add the remaining ingredients and the mushroom stock, simmer for 5 minutes, and strain. Pour into four dipping bowls.

Arrange the noodles in bundles on chilled plates. Scatter the sliced shiitake mushrooms and the enoki mushrooms over the top. Stack the spinach leaves, roll into a sausage shape and cut into four even-sized pieces. Place one spinach portion beside each serving of noodles, with a little mound of preserved ginger. Serve the dressing separately, for dipping.

SERVES 2–4

Onion & noodle salad from Burma

625 g fresh thick egg noodles

1 large onion, cut into
    narrow wedges

½ cup vegetable oil

4 cloves garlic, thinly sliced

1 tablespoon chopped
    dried shrimp

½ teaspoon ground turmeric

3 tablespoons ground dried
    chickpeas (or chickpea flour)

4 soft lettuce leaves

3 tablespoons chopped
    spring onions

3 tablespoons chopped red
    onion or shallot

1½ tablespoons chopped
    roasted peanuts

sprigs of fresh coriander

shreds of fresh red chilli

wedges of lime

DRESSING

2 tablespoons fish sauce

2 tablespoons fresh lime juice

salt and freshly ground
    black pepper

Bring 2 litres of lightly salted water to the boil. Add the noodles and cook for 2–3 minutes, until al dente. Drain in a colander, and set aside.

Heat the oil in a wok over medium heat, and fry the onion until softened and transparent, taking care it does not burn. Add the garlic and dried shrimp, and cook until the onions are deep brown. Remove with a slotted spoon, and spread on absorbent paper to drain. ➤

Sprinkle the turmeric and ground chickpeas or flour into the pan and cook over medium heat until golden. Return the cooked onion mixture and combine well. Pour over the noodles and mix in, then leave to cool. Combine dressing ingredients, seasoning generously with salt and pepper, pour over the noodles and add the chopped spring onion and onion (or shallot). Stir well.

Spread the lettuce on a serving plate. Pile the noodle salad in the centre and scatter with the peanuts, coriander and chilli. Arrange lime wedges around the salad, and serve.

Ground chickpeas give a characteristic nutty taste and add texture to the dish. I have tried using coarsely ground raw cashews, macadamias and roasted peanuts with equal success. Experiment and enjoy!

SERVES 4–6

Chilled noodles with chicken & vegetable shreds

450 g dried somen noodles

450 g skinless chicken
   breast fillet

1½ tablespoons mirin (Japanese
   sweet rice wine)

a few drops of chilli oil

3 small Japanese or Lebanese
   cucumbers, cut into
   matchstick pieces

1 small daikon (icicle radish)
   about 12 cm long, cut into
   matchstick pieces

1 carrot, cut into
   matchstick pieces

½ cup finely sliced
   spring-onion greens

DRESSING

⅓ cup white sesame seeds

1 cup ichiban dashi (page 18)

¼ cup mirin (Japanese sweet
   rice wine)

2 teaspoons fine white sugar

⅓ cup light soy sauce

Boil the noodles in lightly salted water until al dente. Drain, rinse with cold water, drain again, and set aside.

Cut the chicken into 10-mm slices, arrange on a heatproof plate, and sprinkle with the mirin and chilli oil. Set on a rack in a steamer to cook for 15 minutes. Remove and allow to cool.

Arrange the chicken, cucumbers, daikon and carrot around the edge of a large platter and mound the noodles in the centre. Scatter the spring onions on top, then cover and chill.

To prepare the dressing, cook the sesame seeds in a dry frying-pan over medium heat until they smell toasty, then grind in a mortar or spice grinder. Bring the remaining ingredients to a slow boil, reduce the heat and simmer for 3 minutes. Remove from the heat and cool over ice, then stir in the ground sesame seeds. Serve the sauce in individual dipping bowls, with the salad platter in the centre of the table.

You can substitute 1 teaspoon instant dashi stock granules in 1 cup warm water, for the prepared dashi stock.

SERVES 6

Extras

There are all sorts of traditional and not-so-traditional garnishes and accompaniments that complement and bring added flavour and visual appeal to noodle dishes. Here you'll find crisply fried noodle baskets and nests that make elegant edible containers for appetisers or main courses, several simply made classic sauces, and versatile garnishes such as fried onion flakes. There are other suggestions and recipes scattered throughout the book, which you can adopt and adapt as you see fit.

< Cha sui (Chinese roast pork: page 230)

Cha siu (Chinese roast pork)

350 g pork fillet

2 teaspoons dark soy sauce

1 tablespoon light soy sauce

2 teaspoons sugar

2 teaspoons rice wine or dry sherry

2 teaspoons hoisin sauce

½ teaspoon five-spice powder

pinch of powdered red food colouring

Place pork in a shallow dish. Combine remaining ingredients, brush over the pork and marinate, uncovered, for at least 45 minutes. Preheat oven to 220°C.

Place pork on a wire rack in a roasting pan and roast in preheated oven for 20–25 minutes, until the surface is flecked with brown but meat is still pink and moist inside. Slice thinly to serve.

SERVES 4–6 AS PART OF A NOODLE DISH

Fresh chilli sauce

3 fresh red chillies, slit open and deseeded

½ teaspoon sugar

1 teaspoon salt

1½ teaspoons vegetable oil

Chop chillies roughly and place in a spice grinder or mortar. Add sugar and salt with the oil, then grind to a paste.

This dynamite sauce will keep for 3–4 days in the fridge.

Wear gloves when handling chillies – or pay the price!

MAKES ABOUT ⅓ CUP

Noodle baskets or nests

thin or narrow flat egg noodles
vegetable oil for deep-frying

Cook the noodles in boiling water until tender, then drain (but do not rinse).

Heat oil to 190°C. Oil two wire-mesh strainers (one slightly larger than the other). Spread a thin layer of noodles evenly around the inside of the larger one, allowing some of the noodles to loop over the edge if you like. Press the other strainer on top and hold the two handles firmly together as you lower strainers into the oil. Cook until the noodles are golden and crisp, then tip onto a rack over a double layer of paper towel to drain before using.

A custom-made Chinese noodle-nest fryer (available at Asian food stores) lets you make these with ease, but mesh strainers work perfectly well. Dip them into cold oil before lining with the noodles, to prevent the nests from sticking.

Nuoc cham (Vietnamese sauce)

1 fresh red chilli, split open and deseeded

2 cloves garlic, peeled

3 teaspoons sugar

juice of ½ small lime

2½ tablespoons fish sauce or light soy sauce

2–3 tablespoons water

Cut half the chilli into fine shreds and set aside. Cut the remainder into rough pieces, and place in a mortar with the garlic and sugar. Grind to a paste, then squeeze in the lime juice (include the pulp). Transfer the mixture to a bowl, whisk in the fish sauce and water, then add the chilli shreds. (Finely shredded carrot makes an attractive addition.)

 You would never see a Vietnamese table without a bowl of nuoc cham sauce for dipping into, splashing over, and adding its bright flavours to just about any dish. Prepare it fresh for a full flavour burst.

MAKES ⅓ CUP

Peanut sauce for noodles

¼ cup crunchy peanut butter

2 tablespoons light soy sauce

½ cup coconut milk

3 teaspoons freshly squeezed lime juice

2 teaspoons ground coriander

1–2 teaspoons Thai red curry paste, to taste

1 teaspoon sugar

⅓ teaspoon salt

Combine all the ingredients in a saucepan and cook over medium–low heat for 3 minutes, stirring continuously.

Serve tossed through egg noodles for a tangy accompaniment to barbecued or grilled meat.

Substitute macadamia or cashew butter, for a change in flavour.

SERVES 4

Fried onion flakes

225 g shallots
2½ cups vegetable or peanut oil

Peel the shallots and slice very thinly lengthways. Heat the oil in a wok
or deep frying-pan over high heat until hazy, then add the onions. Cook for
1 minute, reduce the heat slightly and continue to fry until the onions are
a deep golden-brown (take care not to burn them). Remove with a slotted
spoon or wire skimmer, and drain on a double thickness of paper towel.

When completely cold, store the flakes in an airtight jar in the refrigerator.
Given the chance, they will keep for many months, but they're so delicious
sprinkled over noodles, rice or curries that they usually don't last more than
a few days.

Tonkatsu sauce

2 tablespoons mirin (Japanese sweet rice wine)

2 tablespoons tomato ketchup

1 tablespoon dark soy sauce

1 tablespoon light soy sauce

1 tablespoon Worcestershire sauce

1 tablespoon Dijon mustard

sugar to taste

Boil the mirin in a small pan until reduced by half. Stir in the remaining ingredients, heat briefly and then allow to cool. Store in the refrigerator.

MAKES ⅔ CUP

Hoisin dressing for chilled noodles

1 tablespoon hoisin sauce

1 tablespoon dark soy sauce

1 tablespoon rice vinegar

2 tablespoons freshly squeezed lime juice

1 tablespoon white sugar

Combine all ingredients, pour over noodles and toss well.

MAKES ½ CUP

Wok omelette

3 small eggs
1 teaspoon vegetable oil

Beat eggs and strain through a fine sieve. Heat oil in a wok, then grease the inside surface with the oil. When the pan is quite hot but not overly so, pour in the eggs and tilt pan to swirl over as wide a surface as possible. Cook until the edges loosen, then flip and briefly cook the other side. Remove to a board to cool, then roll up and cut crossways into very fine shreds.

Homemade egg noodles

2½ cups plain flour

5 medium eggs, beaten

⅔ teaspoon of salt

1¼ teaspoons of white vinegar (optional)

Sift the flour and make a well in the centre. Pour the eggs into the well, and add the salt and vinegar (if using). Work the eggs into the flour, using your fingertips. The dough should be firm, but neither dry nor moist. If you judge that additional egg or liquid is needed, add it before the dough becomes too dry; otherwise it will be impossible to work in smoothly, leaving the dough hard and lumpy in patches.

Knead for 7–10 minutes to make a smooth and elastic dough. Shape it into a ball, dust lightly with flour, place in a bowl, cover with plastic wrap, and allow it to rest for at least 1 hour.

This dough can be used to make fine Chinese-style noodles or wider ribbons, and wonton wrappers. The vinegar helps to soften the dough and cannot be tasted, but it can be omitted if you prefer.

MAKES ABOUT 625 G DOUGH, YIELDING 1 KG NOODLES

Special ingredients

BAMBOO SHOOTS These are available, fresh or canned, from Asian food stores. Canned sliced bamboo shoots suffice for most of these recipes, but fresh shoots have a more pronounced flavour. Store what you don't use in the refrigerator, in a covered container with fresh water. If you change the water daily they should keep for at least a week.

BEAN CURD *see* tofu

BEAN SAUCE, YELLOW Salt-fermented soya beans in a thin, salty liquid, sold in cans and jars. It keeps well, preferably refrigerated in hot weather. White miso is a good substitute, although less salty.

BEAN SPROUTS Sprouts of the mung bean. They should be blanched and refreshed in cold water before using, preferably even for salads. Store fresh sprouts in a perforated plastic bag in the vegetable compartment of the refrigerator for up to 4 days.

BLACAN *see* shrimp paste

BLACK BEANS, SALTED Salt-fermented and dried soybeans, used as a flavouring in Chinese-style dishes. They should be rinsed, dried and chopped before use.

BLACK FUNGUS (WOOD EARS) A crinkly, dried fungus with a crunchy, slightly gelatinous texture. It should be soaked before use, and will expand to several times its original volume. It is now readily available fresh as well.

BOK CHOY One of the most popular Asian greens, with rounded, smooth leaves. 'Baby' bok choy has the best flavour: it cooks in minutes and is best blanched or parboiled before stir-frying.

BONITO FLAKES Fine flakes of dried bonito fish, intensely flavoured and an essential ingredient in Japanese stocks. Make sure it is kept completely dry in storage.

CANDLENUT A dry-textured nut (known as *kemiri* in Indonesia) used to thicken curries, it is similar in taste to macadamias, which can be substituted.

CHILLI-BEAN PASTE Salted soybeans mashed with chilli, salt and occasionally other ingredients (often garlic). A richly flavoured seasoning added to stir-fries and braises.

CHILLI OIL An infusion of vegetable oil with chilli. It is fiercely hot, so use with care. It is available in Asian food stores and some supermarkets.

CHILLIES Dutch red chillies are the most commonly used in Asia, except in Thailand where chilli growing is an art form that has produced a variety of fiery fruits. Deseeding them decreases their heat; to do this, slit along their length and use the point of a small knife to scrape away the seeds as well as the fleshy filaments. Shreds of red or green chilli decorate many Asian dishes. It is best to wear gloves when handling chillies, to prevent skin irritation.

CHINESE CABBAGE (WOMBOK) A large, pale-green, tightly packed Chinese cabbage that is readily available. Common white cabbage can substitute, but its strong flavour will dominate a dish.

COCONUT MILK It is available in cans, compressed blocks, and powdered form. Canned coconut milk varies enormously from brand to brand. When making your selection, shake the can and listen to the slosh of the contents. A thinner milk will splash more noisily than a thicker one, the latter usually better value as it can be thinned with water if necessary. Coconut milk does not keep well, so decant any unused portion into a small container and freeze: add, without thawing, to your next dish.

CORIANDER A small, aromatic herb which is indispensable in all Asian countries except Japan and Korea. The leaves are used for garnish and in sauces; the stems and cream-coloured roots in curry pastes; the seeds in curry-spice mixtures.

DAIKON Also called Japanese or icicle radish, this white tapering root is much used in Japanese cooking. One of the mildest of all radishes, it turns almost sweet and bland when cooked. Available in Asian food stores, it will keep for at least a week in the refrigerator.

DASHI Classic Japanese stock typically based on kombu (dried kelp) and shavings of dried bonito fish. It is simple to make (see recipe on page 18). Convenient forms are also available, such as powder, granules, paste and liquids (follow the manufacturer's instructions).

FISH SAUCE The Thai version is called *nam pla*; the Vietnamese, *nuoc mam*. These two countries use fish sauce as the Chinese do soy, splashing it into almost every dish, dipping into it at the table, and marinating foods in it beforehand. It's salty, pungent, even offensive to the nose, but it imparts a flavour that nothing else can imitate. Keep a bottle on hand, but do keep it tightly capped. Vegetarians can substitute light soy sauce.

FISH/SEAFOOD/SQUID BALLS A puréed paste of seafood formed into bite-sized balls and poached. Look for them in the freezer at Asian food stores, and keep a stock on hand for quick noodle dishes.

FIVE-SPICE POWDER An aromatic Chinese spice combination, traditionally comprising Sichuan pepper, star anise, cloves, cinnamon and fennel. It is both used in cooking, and mixed with salt as a condiment.

GAI LARN Also known as Chinese broccoli, this popular Asian green has round, straight stems with a cluster of leaves at the top and tiny yellow flowers.

Its close cousin, choy sum, has white leaves. They have a slightly bitter taste which is very pleasing.

GALANGAL Known as *kha* in Thailand. A ginger-like rhizome with smooth skin and straight pink sprouts, and a distinctive earthy flavour. Dried and ground to powder, it's usually labelled laos: 1 teaspoon of laos powder gives the intensity of an 8-mm piece of the fresh root.

GARLIC CHIVES Deep green, flat-stemmed members of the onion family, with a distinct garlicky flavour. Thai cooks are particularly fond of them, but a dish does not suffer too noticeably from their absence.

GINGER, FRESH A knobbly, spicy rhizome: choose young ginger, when possible, for its softer, less fibrous texture. If fresh ginger is unavailable, substitute a bottled Japanese or Chinese product. Ground dried ginger does not equate with fresh in most Asian recipes.

HOISIN SAUCE A thick, deep-brown, sweet sauce often served as a condiment. Sold in bottles, it keeps indefinitely in the refrigerator.

KAFFIR LIME LEAF An unusual double leaf that imparts a distinct lemon fragrance to many Southeast Asian dishes, particularly soups and curries from Thailand. It is available fresh, frozen or dried (soak the dried leaf before using): the central rib should be trimmed away if the leaf is to be finely shredded as an edible garnish.

KAMABOKO A cake of minced fish that has been steamed in small log shapes. Its surface is painted with bright pink or yellow food dye. Sliced, it decorates many Japanese soups and hot-pot dishes. Available in Asian food stores.

KATSUOBUSHI Another name for bonito.

KECAP MANIS A thick, sweetened soy sauce used liberally in Indonesian cookery for its rich, deep colour and flavour.

KHA *see* galangal

KOMBU An enormous, tangled kelp that imparts an incomparable 'of the sea' flavour to Japanese stocks and sauces. It is sold dried, usually in 10-cm squares in packs of 6 or so pieces. Rinse surface salt before using. Store dry.

LAOS *see* galangal

LAP CHEONG Hard, dry, sweet Chinese pork sausages with many uses. They are usually steamed for a few minutes before use in a dish, which plumps and soften them. They keep almost indefinitely in the refrigerator.

LEMONGRASS A key ingredient in many Southeast Asian dishes, fresh lemongrass is now widely available. Use only the lower 15–20 cm of the pale-green stem: to release its volatile lemony essence, slit the stem lengthways or bruise with the side of a cleaver. It keeps fresh in the fridge for 1–2 weeks, and can be frozen. If you must use the dried version, soak in boiling water for at least 15 minutes before using. It has a more peppery, less lemony character than the fresh.

LIMES AND LIME JUICE Limes are the key to good Thai cooking. They are widely available, so don't substitute lemon unless you have absolutely no choice.

MAM RUOC *See* shrimp paste

MIRIN A clear, very slightly viscous liquor used in Japanese cooking and sometimes labelled sweet rice wine. If it is unobtainable, a medium-dry sherry works in some recipes, but a closer approximation of flavour and effect would be achieved using sake lightly sweetened with sugar.

MISO This thick, salty paste used in Japanese soups and dressing is made from ground soybeans and salt. It varies from light yellow to a dark red-brown, with a corresponding increase in the intensity of its flavour.

MUSHROOMS Many Asian mushrooms are now available fresh. Shiitake, sometimes called Chinese black mushrooms, have deep grey-brown caps with light cream ribbing beneath. If buying dried, soak for 25 minutes in warm to hot water to soften them before adding to all dishes except those in which they will slowly simmer. The hard stem should be trimmed off close to the underside of the cap.

Enoki: These slender, long-stemmed mushrooms are pale ochre in colour, with tiny caps. Available fresh or canned, they require only very brief cooking. Fresh enoki last only a day or two in the refrigerator.

Oyster: Fragile albino or purple mushrooms with flat caps and off-centre stems, which grow in clusters. They have a subdued wild-mushroom flavour.

Straw: A deep-grey mushroom with a round or pointed head that does not form the traditional cap. Soft-textured and bland, it requires little cooking; button mushrooms can be substituted. Canned straw mushrooms should be decanted and refrigerated, and the water changed every day. Use fresh ones within two days of purchase.

NORI Dark-green sheets of compressed sea laver, used as edible wrappers and as a shredded garnish for many soup and noodle dishes. Store in an airtight container away from light, heat and (more essentially) steam. Hold it briefly over a flame to crisp and brighten its colour before using.

OYSTER SAUCE A thick brown sauce made from dried oysters, whose distinct sea flavour accentuates (rather than overpowering) other flavours in a dish. It is also used as a condiment, particularly on Chinese green vegetables. You can also get a vegetarian version.

PALM SUGAR An aromatic, rich brown sugar, a vital ingredient in many Southeast Asian dishes. It can be replaced with a good-quality dark-brown sugar, but it is usually available in Asian stores and will keep for months, so do stock up on it.

RICE-PAPER SHEETS (VIETNAMESE BANH TRANG) Discs of pale-grey, semi-transparent rice batter. They are softened by immersing in cold water, and used to wrap foods in the same way as spring-roll wrappers.

SAKE A Japanese wine made from yeast-fermented rice. It is clear and not strongly alcoholic.

SAMBAL ULEK A condiment and seasoning made from mashed red chillies and salt, which adds fire to Indonesian dishes.

SESAME OIL An aromatic, nutty-flavoured extract of sesame seeds. It's strongly flavoured, so do not overdo it.

SHICHIMI A seven-spice mixture, probably Japan's most popular condiment. It is sold in small shaker bottles. It contains togarashi (red chilli flakes) with fragments of nori, white and black sesame seeds, hemp seeds, Chinese brown peppercorns and tiny bits of dried mandarin peel. Chilli flakes on their own are an alternative, if you like it hot!

SHRIMP, DRIED Peeled shrimps that are sun-dried to preserve and intensify their flavour. The best will be a bright peach-red colour. Store in a covered container in the refrigerator to maximise freshness.

SHRIMP PASTE A smooth, pungent paste made from fermented shrimps, used as a seasoning. It is known as *mam ruoc* in Vietnam and *kapi* in Thailand. It should be kept tightly sealed, in the refrigerator. The harder, compacted version known as *blacan* is an important seasoning in Malaysia and Indonesia. For best results, wrap in aluminium foil and place in a hot oven or wok for a few minutes before adding to a dish.

SICHUAN PEPPER Aromatic red-brown, peppery berries from the prickly ash tree, which grows extensively in China's Sichuan province. Use with discretion, as an excess has an unpleasant, numbing effect on tongue and lips.

SOY SAUCE Keep both light soy and dark soy sauce on hand. *Light soy* is lighter in colour, sweeter and slightly saltier than dark soy: it is the best soy sauce to use for stir-frying, dressing salads, and braising. *Dark soy* is aged for much longer than light soy, and molasses is added, giving it a brown-black colour, thicker texture and maltish flavour. It is used especially in marinades and red-cooked dishes, and as a dipping sauce.

SOYBEAN PASTE There are several types of soybean paste, seasoned variously with chilli, garlic and spices to provide variations of flavour and pungency. Store bean pastes in the refrigerator in hot weather, and pour a film of vegetable oil over the surface to prevent deterioration.

TAMARIND Tamarind gives an appetising citrus tang to sauces and gravies. It is available as whole seeds compressed into a block, which must be steeped in boiling water, mashed and strained. The simplest form to use is tamarind concentrate, which is sold in jars and can be added directly to a dish.

TOFU Coagulated soymilk, available fresh and processed, and also known as bean curd. *Firm tofu* has been weighted to press out excess water, giving a firmer texture that slices well and does not break up during cooking. *Soft (fresh) tofu* is sold in cakes of about 100 g each. *Silk tofu*, the finest variety, is extremely fragile and must be handled with care. Store in the refrigerator and use within two days, for maximum freshness. *Fried tofu*, available in cakes or cubes, has been deep-fried until the surface is firm and golden. It can be stewed or refried; keeps for several weeks in the refrigerator. *Dried tofu skins* are firm, thin layers that congeal on top of bean curd as it begins to cool and set. They are used as edible wrappers for snacks, particularly in Chinese vegetarian cooking.

VINEGARS, Asian rice vinegars, made from fermented rice (and sometimes other additives), are the most popular type in Asian and Southeast Asian cooking. They are milder and sweeter than most distilled western vinegars (balsamic vinegar is closest in flavour). Chinese vinegars are stronger than their Japanese counterparts, and range in colour from clear to red and brown-black. Chinese *black vinegar* has an intense flavour. *Red vinegar* gets its distinctive colour and flavour from red yeast rice, which is cultivated with a purplish-red fungus. *Japanese rice vinegar* is mildly flavoured and is generally clear to pale yellow in colour. There is a seasoned version used chiefly in sushi and salad dressings.

WAKAME Curly kelp, delicately flavoured and with a pleasing crunch. Japanese use it in salads and soups. Sold dried in small packets, it swells to many times its dry volume when soaked in cold water.

WASABI Root known as Japanese horseradish (though in fact a member of the cabbage family). It looks innocent enough, but has mustard-like heat. It's available as a pea-green paste or powder, the latter generally reconstituted to a paste with water or sake.

WATER SPINACH A Southeast Asian vegetable with triangular, deep-green leaves and long, hollow stems. Known as *kangkong* in Malaysia and Indonesia, *oong choy* in China, and *pak bung* in Thailand, it is available fresh in Asian food stores. Use like spinach, which you can substitute in any recipe.

Conversions

OVEN TEMPERATURES

Celsius (C)	Fahrenheit (F)
150	300
180	360
190	375
200–230	400–450
250–260	475–500

LIQUIDS

Millilitres	Fluid ounces
60 ml	2 fl oz
125 ml	4 fl oz
200 ml	6 fl oz
250 ml	8 fl oz
500 ml	16 fl oz
625 ml	20 fl oz (1 pint)

WEIGHTS

Grams	Ounces
30 g	1 oz
60 g	2 oz
90 g	3 oz
125 g	4 oz
250 g	8 oz
375 g	12 oz
500 g	16 oz (1 lb)
1 kg	2 lb

Index

PENGUIN BOOKS

Published by the Penguin Group
Penguin Group (Australia)
250 Camberwell Road, Camberwell, Victoria 3124, Australia
(a division of Pearson Australia Group Pty Ltd)

New York Toronto London Dublin New Delhi Auckland Johannesburg

Penguin Books Ltd, Registered Offices: 80 Strand, London, WC2R 0RL, England

First published by Penguin Group (Australia), 2008

Many thanks to Freedom Furniture in South Yarra, Matchbox in Armadale,
and Roost in Armadale, for their lovely props.

Cover and text design by Nicholas McGuire © Penguin Group (Australia)
Photography by Julie Renouf
Food styling by Linda Brushfield
Typeset by Post Pre-press Group, Brisbane, Queensland
Scanning and separations by Splitting Image Pty Ltd, Clayton, Victoria
Printed in China by 1010 Printing International Limited

National Library of Australia
Cataloguing-in-Publication data:

Passmore, Jacki.
   Noodle bible.
   1st ed.
   ISBN 978 0 14 300824 8 (pbk.).
   1. Cookery (Pasta). 2. Noodles. I. Title.

   641.822

penguin.com.au